Dedicated to Mia Brophy Quinn and
to those adoptive people who are
looking for their true identity.

Have Faith

2009

Nancy.

Enjoy the story.

Sharon Quinn

AuthorHouse™
1663 Liberty Drive, Suite 200
Bloomington, IN 47403
www.authorhouse.com
Phone: 1-800-839-8640

First published by AuthorHouse   8/19/2008

ISBN: 978-1-4343-8525-3 (sc)

Printed in the United States of America
Bloomington, Indiana

This book is printed on acid-free paper.

Second Beginning

A Story of Adoption

Sharon Lyman Quinn

authorHOUSE®

Contents

Prologue ix

Introduction xi

Circle Drive 1

The Doctor's Daughter. 6

The Island. 11

Name Droppers. 23

Mia's Discovery 31

Revealing Documents 37

Sharing The News. 53

The Letter. 66

A Love Story 82

Unionville. 101

Sisters 108

The Afghan. 118

No Longer A Puzzle 122

Getting On With Her Life. 126

The Best Is Yet To Come 132

Acknowledgements 136

Photo Credits 138

About The Author 139

About The Book

As Mia stood in the parking lot next to her shop, she and a customer discussed what it was like to be pregnant with your first child. Little did Mia know that this woman was her birth mother, and Mia the daughter she gave up for adoption 33 years ago. The baby Mia carried would be the woman's first grandchild.

After her birth in a San Francisco hospital in 1965, a Reno physician and his wife adopted Mia. She was raised with her brother and sisters in a happy loving home. Upon the death of her parents she decided to try and fill the deep longing and emotional gap now present in her life. She began a passionate search for her biological parents in hopes of discovering her medical history. Emotions are on edge as Mia's quest begins, and she encounters files and documents outlining her past history. By daring to intrude into the lives of her birth parents, Mia disrupts an entire family, questions her actions—and uncovers secrets of long ago.

Second Beginning — A Story of Adoption tells the inspiring story of my daughter-in-law's relentless pursuit to uncover her true identity through persistence, love and a great deal of luck. Her story will appeal to readers from all walks of life, especially those who enjoy nonfiction works on personal growth and family issues with spiritual overtones. Mia's story is a positive and uplifting account which will move, enrich and delight the reader.

Prologue

T HE HIGH SCHOOL YEARBOOK rested on the library table. She slowly turned the pages and searched the names under each face in the senior class of 1965. Carefully she scanned the pictures for the name Dupre, the woman's last name. Her right index finger raced over the Ds, her heart pounding in her ears as her left hand tried to steady the shaking pages. It was then that she saw her birth mother's name—a name she had learned only a few hours ago. Staring at the picture, she couldn't believe her eyes. At the adoption agency she had formed an image of the woman's face in her mind. Now she was looking at that same face. It was a face she recognized. Unbelievably, they both knew each other. A life changed in that instant. She was not the same, nor would she ever be. She had made a startling discovery

Introduction

Second Beginning is not a "how to" story for adopted people who want to search for their biological parents. There are so many paths to take and emotions to be dealt with; I would not presume to have the knowledge or skill to advise on any of them. I simply want to share the story of Mia Brophy Quinn, my daughter-in-law. My intent was not to write this as an exposé, but rather as a truthful account of Mia's quest for her birth history. Therefore, I have purposely omitted details about the lives of both sets of parents out of respect for their privacy, as well as the names of the organizations responsible for Mia's adoption.

Mia's story is one of luck, fate and a great deal of irony. A chain of events led to her separation from her biological parents, her existence — unbeknownst to any of them — for 33 years in the same city that they lived in, and their ultimate reunion when she was a grown, married woman. The incidents spurring the search for Mia's birth parents included the passing of the man and woman she will forever refer to as Mom and Dad, Eileen and John Brophy, who adopted and raised her. They will always be a tremendous part of her life and she will love them forever. Mia would not have looked into her birth history had her adoptive folks been alive, especially her mom. After they died, Mia grieved as any child would. Then, following her 32nd birthday, a strong desire to pursue her biological history took hold. Who am I? The thought ran through her mind like a continuous reel of film.

When Mia decided to look for information about her birth history, she felt both excitement and fear, like a person experiencing her first roller coaster ride. The idea of discovering her biological identity was overwhelming at times. Mia has a close-knit group of friends and family who encouraged and supported her, anxious to share in the moment of discovery. Her quest also became a topic of conversation among her peers and customers at Name Droppers Paperie and Gifts, her retail shop. Many of Name Droppers' customers have known Mia for years. They were there when she got married, graduated from college, and had three children. They are well acquainted with her and this story affected many of them deeply.

Mia's story even touched the hearts of total strangers. A few years ago, Mia and her husband Andy were in New York dining at a Manhattan restaurant. They fell into a pleasant conversation with two women at the next table. When the subject of adoption came up, Mia told them her inspirational story. It left them smiling and in tears.

In today's society, stories with happy endings are not abundant. This story is different because the happy ending is Mia's second beginning. The experience with her adoption history has helped Mia establish a positive outlook for both herself and her family. Mia now understands that her past was a hidden beacon, illuminating the path of discovery she needed to take in order to develop and appreciate her future.

Circle Drive

MIA'S DAD, JOHN BROPHY, was an Ear, Nose, and Throat specialist. He completed his residency at Stanford University, served in an M.A.S.H. unit in the Korean War, and then returned to Stanford to teach at the Medical School. He longed to set up a private practice, and within a few years moved to Reno, Nevada, with his first wife and their daughter Patricia. Two more children quickly followed, but the marriage was not to be.

Several years after their divorce, John met Eileen Christy, a beautiful young Canadian convent graduate who worked as a surgical nurse at Washoe Medical Center. They fell in love and were married during the Christmas of 1959. John and Eileen took on the responsibilities of raising John's three daughters; Patricia, Linda, and Sue after a judge granted him

1

custody. When they learned they could not have children, John and Eileen adopted a baby boy. They named him John D'Arcy Brophy—or D'Arcy, as the family calls him.

Two years later, in November of 1965, Mia joined the Brophy family. A family meeting was held in the library, a book-lined room behind the living room. Both rooms shared a huge flagstone fireplace that stretched up to a high ceiling. John had a small fire going and soft music playing as the four children entered the room. The youngsters were barely seated when Eileen exuberantly declared "Our family is going to have our baby girl tomorrow!" She and John were ecstatic. Patricia, Linda, Sue, and D'Arcy bounced off the furniture and jumped on the floor with excitement.

John told the children, in his very serious tone, not to mention to anyone that the baby was being adopted. Back when Linda was adopted, John's mother, a tough Irish schoolteacher, had strong opinions about children born out of wedlock. She felt they were all "unsuitable children," belonging only in orphanages, laundries, or workhouses. They were certainly *not* brought into good Catholic homes. John was so deeply hurt by her statement that he never mended his relationship with his mother. Because of his mother's strong feelings, he decided that only a few select people should know about Linda's, D'Arcy's, or Mia's adoptions.

The next day after school, Linda, Sue, and Patricia ran home as fast as they could. The girls rounded the last corner on Circle Drive to where they could see their home just up ahead, then raced down the driveway. Lula, the family's housekeeper, saw the girls coming and headed them off at the front door. They were sweaty and laughing, anxious to see their new baby sister and trying to guess what she would look like. Lula had her hands full getting them all settled. She helped take off their heavy coats and put their books in a pile on the kitchen table. They tried to calm down as Lula assisted them in washing their faces and hands. Then the girls tiptoed anxiously down the long hall to the master bedroom. D'Arcy joined them, giggling with delight.

Near a velvet chaise lounge was a beautiful white bassinet. The curtains were drawn to darken the room and everyone spoke in whispers. Asleep in the bassinet was their olive-skinned, long- lashed, dark-haired little sister, Mia. Grandma Ga, Eileen's mother, had stayed up all night crocheting the soft pink and white coverlet that now covered the baby. Mia had a little button nose and tiny ears and looked so delicate. The four children were quiet and well-behaved, but soon Mia began to wake up and they had to leave the room.

Within the hour Eileen had carried Mia to the kitchen rocker and was rocking her gently back and forth. All the children wanted to help with the new baby, and D'Arcy was so excited his blond head seemed to pop up everywhere. Patricia, Linda, and Sue were in awe at the array of bottles, formula, and sterilizing equipment that began to fill the kitchen counters. The four children watched in wonder as Ga tested the formula from the baby bottle on the inside of her wrist to make sure the temperature was just right before handing it to Eileen. Wrapped snugly in her blanket, Mia made soft, contented sounds as she began nursing. John, Eileen, Ga, and the children rejoiced at seeing their beautiful baby enjoy her first meal in their home. Mia's life in a cream-colored Cape Cod home on Circle Drive and as the youngest member of the Brophy family had begun.

The Brophy Family
Left to Right: D'Arcy, Eileen, John, Sue, Patricia,
Linda. Mia seated on the floor.
1973

The Doctor's Daughter

MIA HAD A HAPPY childhood. As the children of the Brophy family grew up, the sisters were wonderful to Mia and D'Arcy. They shared their toys and took time out to have fun with their young siblings. When neighborhood children came to play the sisters always found a way to include Mia and D'Arcy in their games. If anything, they indulged the toddlers and went overboard to make sure they were happy. Mia pestered her sisters while they did their homework and pretended to read their schoolbooks, trying to emulate Patricia, Linda, and Sue. She was constantly asking them questions and in return they were patient and loving.

One glorious Christmas Eve in 1972, Mia's dad announced they were all going to visit Ireland in the spring. Just before the family left on their trip, a boy in Mia's second grade class told her she was adopted. The boy had overheard his folks discussing a baby being adopted into the Brophy family many years ago and thought it might possibly be Mia. Adopted, what's that? Mia wondered. Why does he care? She was curious, but not upset because she really didn't know what "adopted" meant. When she arrived home from school that day she told her mother what the boy had said. Her mother confirmed that Linda and D'Arcy were adopted, as was Mia. In a gentle, loving way she explained what that meant. Although it made her think, Mia seemed satisfied and had no further questions.

During their vacation in Ireland, Mia was introduced to many of her dad's relatives. She met countless smiling faces, and thought everyone was nice to her— but from what she understood about adoption, they really weren't her relations...were they? Mia saw that she was treated just like anyone else in the family, so it didn't matter whether a person was adopted or not. It made no difference in the Brophy home and it didn't seem to matter to the relatives in Ireland. After all, three of the five Brophy children were adopted: Mia's sister Linda was the first. Later, Mia asked D'Arcy if he wondered how he became a part of their family. He told her he was never restless or curious about it.

Grandma Ga had always been a huge part of Mia's life. Ga relocated to Reno after a flood on the Russian River took the life of her husband. Their home and all of their belongings were washed away by the raging waters. Ga moved into a condo close by and came to the home on Circle Drive every day to help with the five children. Ga had a loving and gentle nature that the family cherished. She was a strong, stable influence in both Mia's and D'Arcy's upbringing.

Mia did her best to stay out of trouble. She respected her parents and knew the limits of their tolerance. As she grew up she came to understand how her dad's military training and her mom's convent upbringing led them both to conclude that their family needed strict order and discipline. She tried hard with her schoolwork, athletics, and piano studies so her parents would be proud of her accomplishments. Mia was in awe of her dad's medical achievements. In addition to his growing private practice, he brought the Argon Laser to Reno, as well as the cochlear implant method for the inner ear.

D'Arcy and Mia had become their mom's little darlings and she went to great lengths to make them both feel very special. By high school Mia was even beginning to resemble Eileen, with dark brown hair, similar skin coloring, and large, dark brown eyes. When people complimented her mom on having the same appearance and complexion as Mia she always said, "Thank you." Mia never once heard her parents refer to her or D'Arcy as being adopted. In her mom's mind, they really were her biological children.

By Mia's teen years her sisters had all left home to start their careers and search for independence. The family in the house on Circle Drive narrowed down to four, plus their wonderful Grandma Ga, a cat, and a dog.

When D'Arcy became college age he left for Ireland to study with the Pallottine Fathers as a student seminarian. He lived in Dublin where in 1984 he earned his Pontifical Baccalaureate of Sociology. He changed his career choice, returned to Reno, and began his medical studies.

On Mia's sixteenth birthday, she wondered if her birthmother was thinking of her. Does she know that I'm sixteen today? Does she care about me on this special day—or any other day, for that matter? What would my life have been like had she raised me herself? Would she have gotten married or remained single? Would we be living in another city? Her mind was full of these recurring thoughts.

One afternoon during her first year at the university, Mia had just finished practicing the piano when her mom entered the living room and said she had some thoughts she wanted to share with Mia. The two sat down on the sofa. Eileen explained that she and

Mia's dad had taken in several unwed mothers and a battered wife when they were first married. Their family home had extra bedrooms, which provided much-needed privacy. The women were appreciative that they could live out of the public eye in restful and loving surroundings.

Mia's mom said she hoped that if Mia had the opportunity, she would take care of women in a similar situation. Their conversation meant a lot to Mia at the time, and as Mia discovered her own birth history, it had an even greater impact.

Throughout all the years D'Arcy and Mia lived under the same roof, they never discussed being adopted. It was something they never needed to talk about. D'Arcy told Mia he loved his life as a Brophy, and had no desire to find his birth parents. Unlike D'Arcy, Mia always had a place deep inside her where she felt like an imposter. She sometimes sensed a feeling of disconnection from other people around her. My birth mother and birth father are out there, I just know it, was the thought Mia kept tucked away in a corner of her mind—just as you would tuck away a dainty hankie given by a grandmother in the recesses of a dresser drawer for safekeeping.

The Island

JOHN AND EILEEN BROPHY were on a vacation to her home country, Canada. The year was 1963.

In a Victoria, British Columbia, restaurant they happened to meet a gentleman who was going to place his island on the real estate market. After a lengthy discussion, the three agreed to meet at the dock in Sydney Harbor for a boat ride over to the property. It was a warm, sunny day, and the waters were calm as they headed into the Straits of Georgia.

John and Eileen fell in love with the location: the three acres of tall pines, rocky beaches, and languishing seals seemed to be the perfect setting for their family summer holidays. Plans for a modest compound, complete with boathouse, dock, and a rustic one level cabin were drawn up and after minor adjustments, building got underway in late spring.

Every summer after that, John and Eileen's young growing family made the trip to the island they had named Tara. After the boathouse and dock were completed, work began on the cabin. The family slept in tents under the majestic pine trees and listened to the wind rustling in the branches, accompanied by a choir of wildlife sounds. Eileen cooked all the meals on a tiny hibachi. Early morning breakfast tasted so good in the open air, and the delicious aroma of sizzling bacon set a heartwarming tone for the rest of the day's adventures.

The island was Mia's real-life "adventure in paradise." The weather was usually warm and sunny, with a late afternoon breeze off the water that encouraged you to reach for a sweater. There were hidden coves, and a hill behind the house that dropped down to a small cliff just above the ocean. D'Arcy and Mia thought they had discovered their own Treasure Island. There were endless places to explore and intriguing animals to track.

John purchased two boats in Sydney Harbor, a small runaround outboard for D'Arcy and Mia and a larger inboard to accommodate the family, haul building supplies and use on serious fishing trips.

The first building to be erected was the boathouse. John built D'Arcy a small room attached to the boathouse and furnished it with a bunk bed.

The cabin structure was enlarged each summer, but never had electricity or running water. As the years progressed, the rugged island hideaway grew to include two bedrooms, bath, a great room, and a huge deck overlooking the cool ocean and islands beyond. Up behind the cabin were the outhouse and sun shower.

D'Arcy and Mia truly enjoyed exploring the island; it became their way of life for two months every summer. Birds nested in the up stretched pines and roamed the skies. Deer swam back and forth between the neighboring islands and often gave birth to their fawns in the nearby thicket. Adult seals could be heard barking from their perch on the rocks that jutted into the sea while their pups played and fell over each other as they flapped along the ancient, seashell- covered beach.

As a child, Mia would occasionally think about her birth history for a fleeting moment... but it was never mentioned. She felt loved, happy, and at peace with her surroundings. Except for her sister Linda and brother D'Arcy, she never knew anyone else who was adopted.

One of Mia's fondest adventures with D'Arcy happened when a whale surfaced right next to their tiny outboard. The enormous mammal was fabulous to watch, and not until they reported their outing to the family did they realize there could have been serious trouble that day.

Almost before they could walk, Eileen insisted that all the children learn how to swim. This skill, as well as the boat safety John drilled into them as a daily routine, helped make them fearless around water.

Looking back at the brother-sister relationship D'Arcy and Mia shared; one can only imagine what child psychologists who are researching adoption issues would say. The children knew they were adopted but found no reason to ever discuss the subject. Growing up, they each developed strong personal characters that overcame any sadness or loneliness they might have felt from not knowing their biological parents. Under the watchful eyes of their mom and dad, D'Arcy and Mia took care of each other and enjoyed childhood. A psychologist might suggest that deep inside their subconscious, togetherness made them stronger. The common sense and independence they developed gave them a solid feeling of comfort and security.

This all happened in the 1970s, when most people felt safe and protected in a peaceful America that most people today haven't experienced. It wasn't talked about then...it was just a given in everyone's lives. "As parents, Mia and I would never allow that kind of freedom to our three children, but those were more relaxed and more serene times," Andy, who later became Mia's husband, commented, sounding like an older but wiser parent.

It must have been challenging for Eileen when John had to commute back and forth to Reno for his medical practice. During his several week absences, Eileen always had activities planned for the children, such as working on the ever-growing shell collection, nature crafts, puzzles, and building forts in the forest. When provisions ran low and the laundry bag over-flowed, a quick trip into Sydney was in order. The drill was to stock up on supplies at the market, then visit the bakery, on the main street, for treats to take back to the island.

Bath time was down by the pier. Eileen would line the children up and get them wet and soapy; then the children would jump in the ocean to rinse them-selves off. On rare times, they used the outdoor sun shower that hung from a tree behind the cabin. A wonderful contraption, it accumulates rainwater in a plastic drum, then slowly disperses the sun-warmed water when the cord is pulled. The children agreed that lining up on the dock for an ocean dunk was colder but more fun.

They all took turns with latrine duty, the least favorite chore. Even though the family lived in somewhat primitive conditions, they were happy during those summer months, and everyone got along. The older girls read, soaked up rays on the deck, swam, and enjoyed their time away from Reno or at least that's how it appeared to a much younger sister.

As Mia reached her teens, she began to speculate about her adoption history; the thread began to appear on the fringes of her mind. One evening as she sat alone on the pier before dinner, thoughts came to her regarding her birth parents. Had they ever gotten married? Where would they have gone on vacations? Did they have kids like D'Arcy and her, who had a boat and loved to go exploring?

Mia didn't want a "new" family; she just longed to know her true identity. She wanted to be acknowledged by her biological parents and understand why they put her up for adoption. It's difficult to realize you were just "given away," like a puppy or a piece of clothing. How much longer would she have to wait to learn her birth history? She never wanted to approach her mom or dad about this, though, for fear they would think she was unhappy with them.

By Mia's middle school years, her sisters had left home to get on with their own lives. Travel to the island of Tara with three fewer children was much easier. Grandma Ga made several trips there but, she also enjoyed her summers of quiet, back in Reno. Sometimes D'Arcy invited a fishing buddy along for a week of summer angling. The Name Droppers gang came up a time or two, and Jackie Parks, the original owner of the shop, couldn't imagine why anyone would ever want to leave such a peaceful location.

As John got to know Andy, Mia's fiancé, he wanted him to be included in the island vacations. A trip was planned for the summer of 1988 that would include Ga and Andy. His account of that first trip went like this:

"We took the huge ferry over from the mainland to Sydney Harbor on the east side of Vancouver Island, then parked our cars at the Franks' home. The Franks were longtime friends of Dr. Brophy and Eileen's. Then the six of us went to the grocery store for supplies and it was there I saw French labels on food for the first time. Cool! After loading the groceries and provisions onto the boat, D'Arcy, John, and I headed to the bait shop for our fishing licenses and more equipment."

"We all piled into the boat and headed toward the island across smooth summer waters. I remember my first look at that tree covered mound of land with the small cabin, boathouse, and pier. It really was a slice of paradise."

"After unloading the boat, we all pitched in and got the cabin ready for the summer. Shelves were stocked, the propane tank was checked, and ice went into the small fridge and ice chest. John checked to see if members of the native tribes had taken the gifts he always left out for them on the deck, at the end of each summer. There would be hammers, saws, and hand tools of all kinds, along with canned food and blankets. It was a tradition among the islanders to leave provisions for the natives, who would stop at the islands each winter. In all the years they owned the property, the compound was never broken into and John always felt it was safe and in good hands," Andy went on to say.

"My best fish story happened one afternoon after D'Arcy and I had motored into Sydney for a few beers. We started fishing late, on our way back to the island. It was a strike; the fish ran with my line and we heard the unforgettable whirring sound as the reel started spinning. I tightened my grip on the rod."

"The 'knuckle buster' reel was just that. I struggled to get the rod under control and slowly began to reel in the line. About ten minutes later, the fish surfaced right by our boat. The king salmon saw us and dove straight down into the clear dark blue water. We were so excited because we wanted to bring that fish home for dinner. For the next half hour, I was battling the fish. I decided to get a better stance, so I moved from the bow to the stern. But along the way, my foot caught on something and over the side I went, with my prescription sunglasses, baseball cap, and rod."

"My glasses were never to be seen again, the cap floated lazily away, filled up with water and slowly sank, but I managed to hang onto the all important rod. D'Arcy reached out and grabbed it from me while I hurriedly climbed back in the boat. It was getting late; I was sopping wet, and it was cold. I took the rod back from D'Arcy and began to work the fish again."

"I was shivering and watching the dark, churning water for any sign of the fish, when I glanced over and saw D'Arcy getting the net ready for the big catch. The salmon was now swimming close and the next thing I knew, D'Arcy had netted the fish and was tossing it into the boat. In celebration, we blew the horn and rang the bell again and again. Everyone up at the cabin heard, and came running down to the dock to see what all the noise was about. The fish was estimated to be 28 pounds. My biggest catch ever!" Andy said, with his huge grin.

The last island trip we all made was in the summer of 1991. John chartered a 29- foot sail boat named Soldier Wind, and we sailed her north to the Princess Louise Inlet on the Canadian mainland.

Andy said warmly, "John was a great guy. He always had wonderful stories to tell and loved the history of the islands. He had such enthusiasm about the world and the people in it. He went out of his way to make me feel part of the family. I will never forget his kindness."

John retired from St. Mary's Hospital in the fall of 1992, was diagnosed with cancer, and lived for ten short months long enough to see the birth of Mia and Andy's first child, Emmy. Soon after John's death, Ga died in 1993 after a short illness. They both passed away without revealing any clues about Mia's birth history (other than the fact that she was of Greek descent and was born in San Francisco).

Mia had recurring feelings of sadness and loss. She longed for the comfort of a large family to help her cope with those two recent deaths. Even though Andy, Eileen, and Emmy were there for her, an unsettling cloud of loneliness would often hover over Mia.

Over the next few years, Andy, Mia, and D'Arcy brought family and friends to the cabin. Andy and Mia's young niece Makena was a great help with

Emmy. Another generation of fort- builders and shell gatherers found solace and tranquility on the island. One summer, Makena's brother, Mike Scholz, joined with friends Sonny, Kelli, Garrett, and Gabrielle Newman for an island vacation. After a dinner of barbecued salmon and beer, then games on the deck, they all enjoyed sleeping beneath the trees, looking up at the stars.

D'Arcy and Mia inherited the island after Eileen passed away in 1997. She was too tired and sad after her husband and mother died to pass on to Mia the information concerning her birth history.

Andy, Mia, and D'Arcy went to Tara several more times, but eventually realized they would have to sell the island. The Canadian taxes, caretaker costs, and upkeep were more than their modest budgets could justify.

It was very sad when the family turned the island over to the new owners, but they have an ocean full of fabulous memories, and boxes of old home movies, videotapes, and scrapbooks.

Mia knew that someday the time would be right to look for information concerning her birth parents.

The Island
Grandma Ga and Mia

Name Droppers

Mia started working at Name Droppers Paperie and Gifts during the second semester of her freshman year in college. She was eighteen years old with no work experience, but the owner and founder, Jackie Parks, took a chance and hired Mia on the spot. Mia thought Jackie liked the idea that Mia was a doctor's daughter, as Jackie was a doctor's wife.

Jackie had a prime location for her shop, across the front of the Arlington Gardens Mall on West Plumb Lane. She filled her store with upscale paper products, children's items, and beautiful gifts. The mall opened in the mid-1970s when the Junior League of Reno purchased an old, established nursery and transformed it into a dozen boutiques, a restaurant, and an outdoor garden center. While working for Jackie, Mia was exposed to many new faces. Could one of them be her birth mother? It was a thought that occasionally drifted through her mind, even though she was busy with a part-time job and beginning her freshman year in college. Then, on a spring day in 1984, Mia was thrown for a loop when Andy Quinn entered her life.

Andy first saw Mia on the University of Nevada campus. Mia had gone to Bishop Manogue Catholic High School, and had just enrolled in college. Andy asked a mutual friend for an introduction. He was blown away by Mia's smile, and asked her out the next time he saw her. After their casual first meeting, Mia drove home from campus. How does Mia Brophy Quinn sound? she thought with a grin. A few years later they were pinned at the Kappa Alpha Theta sorority house in the traditional Sigma Alpha Epsilon fraternity ceremony. They had a wonderful college romance and balanced party life with work, dating, and studies. Andy soon left his job as a cook at Marie Callender's Restaurant and began working in valet parking at the El Dorado Hotel and Casino.

Andy moved to Las Vegas with his folks after his dad was promoted to Executive VP of First Interstate Bank during the summer of 1987. Andy completed his last year of college and graduated from the University of Nevada, Las Vegas. During those eighteen long months, Andy and Mia became engaged. After numerous trips back and forth, and huge phone bills, the Quinns finally returned to Reno.

Andy never brought up the subject of Mia's adoption. She had told him once while they were dating, but it never affected him or their relationship. "Your life, Mia, is what you make it, and except for medical history, it really doesn't matter," he told her.

Mia had always dreamed of a glorious wedding, and now she had her chance. To her parents' chagrin, she took her spring semester off and put her organizational skills to work. Name Droppers had elegant wedding invitations, announcements, and note cards—everything to make their celebration truly memorable. Soon Mia had her perfect wedding impeccably arranged down to the last detail. Time flew by, and after months of working with florist, musicians, dressmaker, and chef, it was time for the rehearsal dinner and the exciting day to follow.

The evening before her wedding, Mia's folks called her into the library and said they thought the time had come to tell her of her heritage. Outside of telling her she was born in San Francisco, this was the first her parents had ever mentioned any details of her adoption. As Mia waited anxiously, just two facts emerged. Her parents told her she was of Greek descent and born in San Francisco. She wanted to know more, but decided to wait until after she was married.

Their September 1988 wedding was amazing—everything Mia had planned for and more. Mia and Andy entertained over 300 guests at a dinner and dance reception at the Hidden Valley Country Club. After returning from a magical Caribbean honeymoon, they moved into their first home, an apartment near the Truckee River. Mia returned to school that spring semester and continued her job at Name Droppers.

After Andy had worked at First Interstate Bank for a year, management decided they wanted him to get some experience at their branches in Las Vegas. Moving to southern Nevada was an adventure for Andy and Mia. It was the first time either of them had been away from family. They found a new apartment and renewed past friendships. Mia got a job at Bullock's and enjoyed working alongside her wonderful boss, Tova Allen. Tova was a former showgirl and had lived in Vegas for years. She told Mia thrilling stories about the casino entertainment world during the memorable 1950s and 1960s. When Mia began her classes at UNLV, she decided to leave her retail job and began working as a part-time bank teller with First Interstate Bank.

While living those eighteen months in Las Vegas, Mia sometimes found herself glancing at faces, wondering those same thoughts about discovering her birth parents. She remembered her mom saying that D'Arcy was born in Las Vegas. Could she have been born there, too? She would occasionally catch herself looking closely at customers for features similar to her own—hair color, facial structure, and brown eyes. Then she would stop herself when she realized what she was doing. Her imagination was at it again. Mia suspected that the feeling of unrest she had might never go away until her birth parents were found.

After the bank transferred them back to Reno, Mia finished up her remaining classes and graduated from college at UNR. She then spoke with Jackie, the owner of Name Droppers, about returning to work. Jackie was delighted to have Mia back. Mia felt fortunate to have experienced the two jobs in Las Vegas, as they helped confirm her decision to return to Name Droppers. The idea of working in a small, independent store appealed to Mia. Merchandise selection and display were at the owner's discretion, with no corporate interference, and the customer-owner relationships were important in order for a small business to succeed. Mia strived to treat the clientele in the same manner she enjoyed being treated. Personal attention, a smiling face, and time to answer their questions were her goal. In 1991 Jackie promoted Mia to store manager. Mia felt grown up, responsible, and proud knowing that Jackie would entrust her with her exquisite shop. Jackie had taught Mia the ins and outs of running a retail business and had given Mia the confidence to one day own her own store.

Being independent and her own boss had been a dream of Mia's since she started working at Name Droppers. Often Mia read about women who owned their own flower shops, bookstores, and boutiques. Articles in publications like *Victoria Magazine* featured inspirational stories of women who were successful in the small retail business world. So, several years later when Jackie announced that she wanted to retire, Mia got her chance to be one of those women. She and Andy decided to purchase the store. Jackie was thrilled to have Mia carry on the tradition of personalized attention her customers had come to expect, and Mia was happy to take over such a well-loved and highly respected institution.

Mia and Andy's first child, Emmy, was born in 1993, followed by their second daughter, Gilly, two years later. With added responsibilities at work and the purchase of their first house, Andy knew Mia could use some extra help at home, so they hired a babysitter for the girls. Andy left the bank to become a stockbroker and moved to downtown Reno to manage the Wachovia Securities office.

During those years at Name Droppers an occasional hum could be heard from one of the customers in the store. She quietly roamed through the four connecting rooms, always humming to herself as she shopped. Who was this lovely, unassuming woman? Amongst themselves, Mia and the staff called her "The Hummer." She was an elementary school teacher. She shopped at the store often, and was always very pleasant. It would be several more years before Mia would discover this woman's remarkable identity.

Mia and Andy
Wedding day, September 1988, Reno, NV

Mia's Discovery

FOR YEARS MIA WONDERED who her birth parents really were. Perhaps someone who couldn't take care of a baby and had to give her away? Or maybe they had both died and had no family. Later, when Mia learned about boys and dating, she thought maybe her birth mother had gotten "into trouble" as they used to say, and had put her up for adoption.

A year before Mia's mom died she gave Mia an old, yellowed letter she found while going through family papers. Written in 1965, it was from Family Agency. Mia had learned three years earlier that Family Agency of Nevada had arranged her adoption in the fall of that same year. It began: *Dr. and Mrs. Brophy, here is the information you requested about the baby girl we placed in your home....* The contents were very general. The letter noted that the birth father was of Greek ancestry and the mother was Welsh; however, it provided no names or details. Mia was intrigued, but cautioned against asking her mom any sensitive questions. Mia did not want to seem overly anxious for more information for fear she would hurt her mom's feelings. She was patient and felt that more disclosure would follow in time. Sadly, it never happened.

Two Christmas seasons came and went without either of Mia's parents or her delightful Grandma Ga. Though Mia had her loving husband, children, family and friends for comfort and security, the pain of missing her parents and grandma was almost unbearable and was accentuated during the holidays. As Mia grew up, her mom always made Thanksgiving and Christmas huge, memorable events. Decorations, presents, lights, music and wonderful meals were her favorite gifts to her loved ones. Another beloved tradition was a Mexican Posada. The entire family would parade down the driveway, each holding a candle. They approached the front door, then asked Ga, the innkeeper, if there was any room at the inn. This Mexican Posada is a tradition Mia continues every Christmas Eve with her family to this day.

At a dinner party Mia and Andy attended in early January, a friend mentioned an acquaintance who had recently found her biological parents. Almost jokingly, Mia thought to herself, "Cool, I'll do it, too!"

It was shocking for her to realize that she could now entertain the idea of actually beginning to look for her medical history. This was the first time she felt comfortable with the idea—free from the worry of hurting her parents' feelings.

Mia's parents loved each other deeply and enjoyed going to marriage encounter workshops. At these workshops they were encouraged to keep notebooks in which to write down their thoughts about each other. In one of these books archived in the family history file, Mia's mom wrote: *I wish I could thank the woman who gave Mia to me.* These warm and touching words gave Mia the confidence she needed to move forward. She felt now that she might have a hand in creating her own destiny.

One day at work Mia accessed the Internet and found a service that could track a person's background and could also determine if anyone was looking for a person. The service required ordering a packet, but after it arrived in the mail a week later, Mia decided she didn't want to use their method. She just couldn't motivate herself to fill out the paperwork, then send it in to learn whether a birth parent or sibling was trying to find her. It felt too much like entering a contest. Would she be the winner? Mia put the packet away.

It was then that Mia decided to phone Family Agency to inquire about basic guidelines she needed to apply for adoption information. The phone was answered by the kindest voice Mia had ever heard, and one she will always remember. Mia explained who she was and why she was calling. The woman on the phone retrieved a file, and within seconds Mia discovered that the mysterious details of her life actually existed in an office just a few miles from her home. She wanted to reach through the phone and take the file off the woman's desk.

The social worker said her name was Peggy. She explained what paperwork Mia would need to bring to the office if she wanted her to research the history of Mia's adoption. "The first thing," she said, "is to get a notarized letter stating who you claim to be. Our office will only be able to give you general information."

From that point on, Mia would be on her own to seek access to court records which, most likely, would be sealed. The whole process sounded involved, but worth the effort. It brought back childhood memories of working on a puzzle for hours only to discover the last few pieces were missing. This time I'm going to find the missing pieces, Mia thought.

After the conversation with Peggy, Mia just sat at her desk and stared at the phone, stunned. She took a deep breath and reached for a bottle of aspirin staring at her from the shelf behind the store computer. "I may need a case of these pills before my research is over," Mia said to herself out loud, swallowing a swig from a water bottle.

Mia had passed through the rites of growing up—confirmation, communion, dating, getting a driver's license, and graduating from college—with her adoptive parents, "Mom" and "Dad." She was now a married mother of two and the owner of a small business. Mia had a good life and was thankful for her growing family. Still, like so many adopted children, curiosity about her origins had gnawed at her for years. It was sometimes a nibble, sometimes a bite, but it never released its grip.

After Emmy was born, Mia's pangs of curiosity about her birth parents deepened. Mia's mom had told her that she had suffered from cystic fibrosis as a child. Soon after that eye-opening and frightening disclosure, Mia had Emmy genetically tested. Mia vaguely remembered being sick in bed, but she didn't realize the seriousness of her illness. She wondered what else her mom hadn't remembered to tell her. When her second daughter, Gilly, was born, Mia's frustration only worsened. Emmy was a healthy baby, except for a few ear infections. Gilly was also prone to ear infections and had occasional bouts with asthma. Was that it, or could there be more medical problems ahead that were related to hidden genes?

Would there be artistic or musical talent to encourage? Mia had no way of knowing. It was a help-less feeling, but she knew she was not alone in her thinking. What about the thousands of adopted adults who were now parents and knew next to nothing of their own genetic history?

The sense of loyalty Mia felt toward her parents had held her back from reaching out for her roots. Perhaps if she had been brought up in an unloving, abusive home, she might have felt an urgent need to ask questions concerning her adoption. But she didn't. Not wanting to seem like a Pollyanna, Mia, for the most part, had been content. But now she had a family, and there were genetic and medical issues to consider. With nothing holding her back and no feel-ings to hurt, Mia was ready to pursue her past—to satisfy her own lifelong curiosity, but first and fore-most to be a responsible parent. Her mind was set and she was comfortable moving forward.

Revealing Documents

IT WAS A CRISP, spring-like day approaching the end of an unusually mild winter in Reno. The year was 1999. Flower bulbs were pushing their way to the surface in the yards around town. Mia loved this particular time of year. It held a special occasion for her, the day just before her mom's birthday and was a celebration Mia had marked since she was a little girl. It was a Thursday, errand day, the day she took off from the gift store.

Andy had left early for work. As usual, Mia got six-year-old Emmy and Gilly, age three, ready for school. She drove down tree-lined Plumas Street and headed up to northwest Reno. After she dropped the girls off at Lion and the Lamb Christian School, she sat alone in her car, overcome by a sudden onslaught of emotions. Her heart felt heavy and a strange sadness filled her to the core.

Each year as the end of February approached, the thoughts of what she would get her mom and Grandma Ga for their birthdays filled her head. Mia drove back home. She completed the morning housework and prepared to leave on errands. Suddenly, there it was again—the damp, unsettling feeling of loneliness and gloom whispering, "Who are you, who are you?" She felt frightened, and a sense of urgency flooded her heart and mind.

Mia rushed to her desk drawer and retrieved an envelope. It was the notarized letter she had secured after talking with Peggy at Family Agency. Now was the time. She needed to act on her own feelings. "Do something. Don't just think about it again, do something!" she told herself out loud.

The letter read: *My name is Marie Louise Teresa Brophy (Quinn). I was adopted November 11, 1965, through Family Agency. I was born in San Francisco. I am interested in obtaining any information that could assist my search in the circumstances of my adoption.*

Mia put the letter in her purse, got into her car, and drove off. She grabbed some lunch, then stopped at the shop and told her manager, Carol York, that she was in charge for the day. Then she headed off with her list of things to do.

As part of her yearly physical, Mia needed to drop by the blood lab near Saint Mary's Hospital, just a few blocks west of downtown. As she approached the medical center, she glanced at the original section of Saint Mary's. It was a lovely old tan, stone, and stucco building surrounded by mature trees and rosebushes. She could see the window of her dad's office where he had served as Hospital Administrator after retiring from his medical practice. Sadly, he wasn't behind that window anymore. She didn't stop. For some reason she felt detached from her body, as though she was watching herself drive away from the hospital.

Suddenly, the lab was no longer on the agenda, nor was the grocery store, nor the Meadowood Mall. When the car came to a stop, she found herself over a mile from St. Mary's, in front of the Family Agency building. "This is it," she told herself. "Now or never." Mia was as ready as she would ever be. She opened the car door, got out, and walked toward the front of the ageing building. She moved quickly and with purpose, holding her head high. She had gotten this far and was feeling proud of herself. Don't stop now, she thought, trying to fill her mind with encouraging thoughts.

Once through the front door, Mia followed a sign pointing the way down a hall toward the Family Agency office. She was surprised by the sparseness of the office. She entered a simple reception area separated by partitions defining individual work areas. As she approached, Mia saw a woman sitting behind the reception desk talking with another lady. They appeared busy and involved in deep conversation.

Interrupting them, Mia excused herself, smiled, and asked for Peggy, the social worker she spoke with on the phone just a few weeks ago.

"Good morning," said the woman standing beside the desk. "I'm Peggy."

She had a pleasant smile and her voice had a touch of familiarity. Mia introduced herself.

"I can't believe you're here," Peggy said. "I just had your case file on my desk."

Coincidence? Mia wondered.

Peggy was a warm, welcoming person with short, reddish hair. She said it was curious that Mia had stopped by because it so happened she had spent the morning copying the basic information from Mia's file and was planning to save it in a separate folder to give to Mia when she came in the office. Strange coincidence, indeed, Mia thought. Weeks had passed since she had called to inquire about her birth history, but there Peggy was, working on it. She could not have known Mia was coming on this very day.

Peggy asked Mia to join her in an office just down the hall. Mia couldn't believe this was happening! She followed with tunnel vision. Peggy motioned for Mia to sit down, then pulled another chair around and sat in front of her desk. They sat close, face-to-face. Mia's hands were trembling so much she had to lace her fingers together to steady them. Up until then Mia had been absorbed in the moment, not thinking ahead about possible outcomes. Suddenly, in a rush, she felt herself jarred into reality. What in heaven's name was she doing here?

Mia reached into her purse, pulled out the notarized information, and handed it to Peggy with a shaky hand. Peggy glanced at the letter, scrutinized it briefly, and seemed satisfied. She placed it on her desk and proceeded with a short interview.

"Why are you interested in looking for your birth parents?"

Mia explained that her mom and dad had passed away. She said that, from a health standpoint, she wanted to learn her biological parents' medical histories. Should she, for example, be concerned about the possibility of herself or her children developing a major illness? Having been raised in a doctor's home with a former nurse as her mom, she had been taught the importance of preventive medicine.

The more they talked, the more Peggy determined that Mia had no hidden agenda. She was not after anyone's fame or fortune. Mia knew that the social worker was giving her a final screening, and tried to answer her questions as succinctly as possible. Peggy then asked how many children Mia had and what she knew about her adoption history. Mia told her she had been born in San Francisco and adopted by Dr. and Mrs. John Brophy, that her birth father was of Greek heritage and her birth mother's heritage was Welsh.

Peggy stood up, walked to a closet behind the desk, and opened a huge filing cabinet.

So many people's histories are sitting in those drawers, just like mine, Mia thought.

Peggy took out a large, two-inch-thick manila file. She explained that it held assorted bits of information, including newspaper clippings about Mia's adoptive parents and the circumstances of her adoption. A thinner file was next to the computer. Mia would soon discover that this file contained the histories of her biological parents.

Peggy picked up both files and sat down next to Mia. "I will give you some general information," she said, "but I won't be able to tell you any last names or your birth parents' whereabouts." Such information, she told Mia, was sealed by the court to protect the birth parents' privacy. Mia wondered how many other adopted children had heard a similar statement from social workers all over the country.

Mia was wide-eyed. She never imagined that the answers to all her questions could be found in a social services office in the very town where she lived. Mia had imagined that these kinds of secrets were stored in dark basements behind thick, locked doors, accessed only by an exclusive code entered into a panel of flashing lights, in cities far away. She had never talked with a person who had found a birth parent or discussed the involved process it took to reveal the truth. How was she to know? Just how many answers was Peggy willing to reveal?

Mia's mind raced. Hundreds of thoughts rushed in and out. One in particular kept intruding loudly: The information Peggy held in her hands was part of her life. She had Mia's history *right there* in those worn, cream-colored files. Mia's hands started to tremble again, so she laced her fingers together once more and squeezed them even tighter. A feeling of entitlement mixed with vulnerability welled up inside of her. She also felt the familiar pangs of guilt she often experienced when entertaining the pursuit of her birth history. Mia always thought questions about her adoption would upset her folks, but she only assumed this emotion. Now her parents were both gone and so she could not hurt their feelings, she reminded herself. But she felt guilty anyway.

As she fought to keep herself under control, Mia realized she was not the least bit aggressive as she feared she might be, tempted to grab the files that held the secrets to her past and run out the door with them. Adopted children are accustomed to a feeling of powerlessness resigned to the fact that unknown circumstances often rule, their lives. Sometimes Mia thought it unfair that she was not allowed to be privy to her life's most intimate details. Someone else had control.

Peggy opened the first folder and carefully began turning the pages that were bound together at the top by a large metal clip. She rested it carefully on her desk, the pages open and almost flat as she began to explain, "Your mother's name was Pamela, your father's name was Angelo, but people called him Chris."

Mia noticed that Peggy did not seem overly protective of the file. She did not hold it in a concealing way or try to cover up parts of it with her hands. As Peggy spoke, Mia glanced down at the exposed tab that labeled the file. She was stunned to see that she could make out the black, clearly-written letters. Mia instantly felt guilty and her heart once again started to pound. She felt like she was back in school and had just cheated on a test by stealing a glance at her neighbor's paper. Mia looked away quickly and tried hard not to gaze back again, but she knew she couldn't resist. The history of her birth and the years that followed were in this file, and a name sat before her just waiting to be read. Mia's eyes returned to the telling black letters. After seeing them, she had a great deal of trouble focusing on Peggy's words. Peggy was going on and on about her case, but Mia didn't seem to hear.

The letters read: DUPRE, PAMELA GALE.

That's my mother's name! Oh, my God...that's my mother's name! Mia thought. She wanted to ask Peggy about it, but she didn't dare. Her mind reeled. No one but an adopted child could know how Mia felt at that exact moment. The thrill of identifying with someone out there in the world who was your blood relation was euphoric. Mia had just discovered another piece to the puzzle that made up her life.

Mia had always wondered about the physical characteristics of her birth mother. Was she plain or pretty, tall or short, slim or pudgy? Now at last she had her first concrete evidence about her birth mother's existence. The name looked French to Mia. She kept saying it over and over in her head so she wouldn't forget it. After all, she certainly couldn't take out her pen and jot it down on a piece of paper in front of Peggy. She *had* to remember.

Peggy continued on about Mia's birth parents' history, and Mia finally began to focus on her explanation. Their first names were Chris and Pamela. They were both from Reno. They were 18 and in high school when Pam had gotten pregnant. Peggy went on to tell Mia that since they were still in school and too young to get married, both families felt the best course of action was to put the baby up for adoption. Chris had come to America from Greece when he was just a few months old. He had a large family with four brothers and three sisters. The file said he was very athletic in high school.

I'm athletic, too, Mia thought.

"Oh, look," Peggy said. "It says here he was in the military." She flipped a page over and tilted the file toward Mia for a moment, revealing a form he had filled out to approve the adoption.

In a flash Mia glanced at a large black signature: ANASTASSATOS, CHRISTOS ANGELO. Mia tried to control her breathing. She just knew Peggy could hear her heart pounding. Anastassatos? That last name was very familiar to Mia. Her husband had known an Anastassatos at Reno High. They were a large, respected Reno family. Peggy told Mia that Pam had gone to San Francisco to give birth to her and that Chris had paid the bill for the birth and arranged for the adoption.

Peggy closed the thick file, placed it on her desk, and picked up the second one she held on her lap. She described how John and Eileen Brophy had adopted a son through Family Agency with the help of their good friend, Father Shallow, two years before Mia's adoption. The son, of course, was Mia's brother, D'Arcy.

"Mrs. Brophy called the office," Peggy began as she read from the notes in the file. "She explained over the phone how she and her husband had adopted a son and were now interested in adopting a daughter, preferably with dark hair and brown eyes like her own."

That sounds like my mom, Mia thought warmly. It was as though she had called Neiman-Marcus to describe a coat she wanted to order.

Peggy went on to say that within a few months, the agency told Mia's mom and dad they were receiving a baby girl who fit that description. The child had just been born in San Francisco and was under the custody of the State of California. Arrangements were immediately made for the newborn to be released to the State of Nevada and brought to Reno on a bus.

Peggy said, "Mrs. Brophy came into the office by herself, picked up the infant and went home. Dr. Brophy couldn't get away from work and said he would leave the decision up to his wife."

Initially, no papers were signed to obtain Mia. The Brophys had gotten help from some influential friends within the community, including Father Shallow. They had local officials call the agency. The social workers understood it was a done deal and were told the Brophys were a wonderful couple who loved children and would provide a fine home for the baby girl. Mia's mom once told her that her adoption had created a slight uproar because another family had been in the process of trying to adopt Mia. Fair? No, but her parents' years of work and dedication to the community gave them an edge. It also helped that Mia's dad and Father Shallow had served together on volunteer boards and were the best of friends. In fact, Father Shallow often had dinner at the Brophy home.

As Peggy turned over several more pages in the file, she read Mia a letter about a home-check the agency had conducted after the first month of her adoption. It told of Mrs. Brophy hiring a woman who came to the house every day to help with the children and housekeeping. It also mentioned Mia's older sisters, as well as D'Arcy. The home-check was successful and stated that Mia was to be permanently placed with the Brophy family. Mia thought it was wonderful that the agency kept such consistent records. These accounts showed not only her history, but gave her a timeline throughout her whole adoption process.

At the end of the file, on the last page, was a yellowed newspaper clipping that revealed that Mia's biological parents, Pam and Chris, had eventually gotten married. Wow! Mia was floored. This meant she could have actual biological brothers and sisters! Growing up she had her older sisters, a few cousins, aunts, uncles, and grandparents, but there was always an ineffable barrier—except with D'Arcy. It was the realization they were her relatives, yet not her relatives.

As Mia tried to process all of the information flooding her head, her brain suddenly cleared and formed an equation, merging her birth mother's name, Pam, with her birth father's surname, Anastassatos. Oh my word, Mia thought. Pam Anastassatos. I know her! I know her! She's the lady who shops at Name Droppers—The Hummer!

Mia always noticed The Hummer when she shopped at the store because of her pleasant humming. She tried to clear her head enough to put the face with the name, but she knew she needed more confirmation. She couldn't believe it would be this easy—that this person, someone she knew, might be her biological mother. Mia began to recall a gentle-faced, thin, attractive, dark-haired lady with fair skin. Could this be the woman who had given birth to her?

Peggy stood up with the file and walked around to the back of her desk, where she casually laid it down on top of the first file. She seemed unaware that Mia had noticed the names written on the labels as she suggested ways for her to continue her search. "Old school yearbooks are a good place to start," she said. "Look for first names and faces that might resemble you."

Mia wouldn't have too hard a time. After all, in 1965 there were but three public high schools and one Catholic school in the neighboring cities of Reno and Sparks.

Peggy handed Mia some literature on how to deal with her emotions during her upcoming investigation, and gave her the name of the Washoe County district court judge who would be most amenable to opening the sealed court files. Mia thanked Peggy profusely and shook her hand. As Mia stood up, she thought she must have a strong heart to have survived the last hour in a state of constant panic—and sturdy knees to still be able to get up off the chair.

"Will you keep in touch and let me know how your search goes?" Peggy said with her soft voice and warm smile.

"Absolutely," Mia said.

As Mia left the office and walked to her car, she wondered in her heart if Peggy had wanted her to see those names printed on the file. She guessed she might never find out. She wondered, was Peggy as generous with other adoptive people, or was it just Mia's case? Was there something printed in her file that said if she started asking questions it was all right for the agency to give her some helpful hints and direction? Peggy, knowingly or not, had just shown Mia a part of her life she might never have discovered on her own. Could it really be this easy? She felt that her entire birth history had just fallen into her lap.

Mia was totally exhausted when she got back into her car. She had been there only an hour, but time had become irrelevant. She felt dazed, but her heart was still in place and beating louder than a drum in a marching band. She knew she had to be home by 4 p.m.; her babysitter would have picked up the girls from daycare by then. She had a few hours left.

While she sat in her car deciding what to do next, she called Andy from her cell phone. His assistant answered and said he was on a long distance call with the corporate office and wasn't available. So Mia drove to her in-laws' home to share the exciting news.

Sharing The News

Mɪᴀ's ᴍᴏᴛʜᴇʀ-ɪɴ-ʟᴀᴡ Sʜᴀʀᴏɴ ᴡᴀs in her living room reading the latest Patricia Cornwell novel on that February afternoon. She waved when she saw Mia coming up the brick walkway opened the door, and invited her in.

Mia just looked at her and said, "Sharon, I know who I am."

Sharon looked back at her, puzzled, not really understanding what she meant. Then she smiled and said, "That's great, Mia." Seeing Mia's excitement, Sharon asked, "Mia, you seem so keyed up. What happened? Is there anything wrong?" She always had questions, and didn't fail Mia now. But before she could go on, Mia couldn't contain herself and just unloaded all her emotions. As they walked into the living room, she explained what had transpired during the past hour.

Mia asked if David, her father-in-law, had any yearbooks from Reno High.

"Yes," Sharon said. "Help me move the piano. They're behind the doors here in the bookcase."

Sharon removed four yearbooks from the shelf, the classes of 1954-1958, and placed them on top of the piano. Getting more energized by the minute, they each picked up a book and turned to the index section.

"What are their names? Who are we looking for?" Sharon asked.

As Mia revealed the names of her biological parents, Sharon had no response to the name Pam Dupre, but recognized the Anastassatos name immediately. She was both stunned and happy at the same time. She and David were friends with several members of the Anastassatos family. Then her expression changed from amazement to confirmation. "I knew it, I just knew it," she told Mia eagerly. "Back when you and Andy were first dating, and after he told us you were adopted, I remarked to David that you must be an Anastassatos. Your looks, the timing—it all fit. I've told him that several times."

Sharon had never mentioned this to Mia. Something had always kept her from telling both Mia and Andy about her belief—and really, she hadn't any proof. It was just a hunch.

Sharon immediately got on the phone and called David at his Wachovia Securities office in downtown Reno. She gave him a brief update on what was happening. He was totally amazed and rattled off most of the first names in the Anastassatos family he could remember, and suggested Sharon take a look in the phone book. She found Pam and Chris listed, but only their phone number, not their address. As Mia continued leafing thorough the yearbooks, she discovered their names were missing. She and Sharon decided they must be younger and included in later yearbooks, which David didn't have.

Mia glanced at her watch. It was 3:30 p.m. Reno High classes had been out for almost an hour and Mia wanted to look for more yearbooks in their library. Hurriedly, she said goodbye to Sharon, jumped in her car, and drove down the hill. As Mia sped away, Sharon saw only the blur of the white Explorer and her license plate, which read "Mama Mia."

Mia arrived at the school a few minutes later. She parked in the circular driveway in front of the main two-story brick building, then rushed through the double doors and entered the rotunda. She asked a passing student for directions to the library. Having gone to Manogue High, Mia was a stranger in the halls of Reno High.

She walked quickly to the library. On the way she encountered a few mothers who were customers at her shop. She waved and said "hi." As she reached the library and opened the door, she could see that the librarian was about to leave.

"May I please have five minutes? It's very important," she pleaded.

For all of her outer calm, the woman must have sensed Mia's excitement. "Of course," she said. "How can I help you?"

Mia asked the lady if she could show her the section where the yearbooks were archived. The librarian guided Mia to the shelves, where Mia selected the 1965 yearbook, the year of her birth. Mia quickly pulled out a chair and sat down at the closest table. She searched the index under the A's but could not find Chris Angelo Anastassatos. Her hands were clammy and shaking, and her pulse thundered through her head as she carefully turned each page, searching the yearbooks two years before and after 1965—with no luck.

Next Mia looked for the name Pam Dupre in the 1965 yearbook. To her amazement, it was listed in the index. Her heart fluttered and her face was hot and prickly as she stared at the name. Mia flipped back to the pages in the Senior Class section, and scanned each page under the Ds. Her throat was dry and she wished she had brought along the water bottle from the car. Then she saw the print that read "Pamela Dupre"—her birth mother—a name she had learned just a few hours ago. Mia looked down at the picture with both confirmation and amazement. This was the same face she had pictured in her mind at Family Agency. This woman was her birth mother. There was the proof, right in front of her—a photo of a young woman with short hair and a warm smile. Mia had found her biological mother after all these years.

Mia recognized Pamela Dupre the second she saw her photo. She had been in Reno all along, living her life not far from Mia! Tears and excitement filled Mia to overflowing. Then she felt a wave of shock and disbelief. Underneath the photo was a list of her birth mother's activities. They were: Homecoming Queen Candidate and Social Club Member. Like mother, like daughter, Mia thought. She had been a member of her homecoming court at Manogue and was oh, so social. After wiping tears off the page with her Kleenex and gathering her emotions, Mia glanced around the room in search of the librarian, who waited patiently at her desk.

Mia asked her, "Could I please check out several of these yearbooks?"

She was anxious to take them home to show Andy, and to scour the pages for any further information on Pam. Deep inside she felt a passion to find the truth. Mia didn't want to reveal her reasons to the librarian as to why she was so interested in the yearbooks. Reno was still a small city in so many ways. Between the two families, they knew many people, and Mia wasn't yet ready to share her secret.

"I'm sorry, but it is against school policy to check out the annuals. They must stay in the library," the librarian told Mia.

"Please," Mia said. "It would mean so much to me if I could borrow them." She was willing to give up a credit card or driver's license—anything to provide collateral.

The librarian looked at Mia's teary, blotchy face, and said, "This seems important to you. Let's go ask the principal."

They hurried along the halls that led to the office of Mrs. Alan Ross. Jan Ross and Mia's mother-in-law had been friends since college at UNR—a fact Mia learned from Sharon later on. Reno was a small town, indeed.

Upon arriving at the principal's office, they found one of Mia's store customers visiting with Mrs. Ross.

"I know Mia, she'll bring the books back," Mia's customer told the principal, vouching for Mia.

The principal agreed to Mia's request, and Mia thanked her for making an exception to school policy. She happily took the 1963-1965 annuals and prepared to go home.

"I promise you I'll have them back by three o'clock tomorrow," she said, leaving a credit card with the librarian.

Mia's mind was in a misty haze, and she knew she would have to drive home carefully. Pulling into the driveway of their Cape Cod-style home a few minutes later, Mia could see Rose, her babysitter, getting ready to leave. Emmy and Gilly greeted Mia at her car. They waved good-bye to Rose, and then went inside.

Four, four-thirty... time crept by as Mia waited anxiously for Andy to get home. He left the house at dawn every morning and usually arrived home by late afternoon. When he walked through the front door, it was five o'clock. Mia hit him with her news all at once—she just couldn't stop talking. From then on, the evening was filled with tears, electricity, questions and answers. Even the girls could feel the excitement in the air. Mia proudly showed Andy Pam's pictures in the yearbook. He had never seen her before. He was just starting to absorb the fact that Mia had actually found her birth mother and that they were looking at her photograph.

David and Sharon called to see how they were doing and to see what Mia had found out. They asked if she had located Chris in any of the yearbooks from the school library. Mia told them Chris must have gone to a different school or was there at a different time. They were puzzled but thought he might have gone to Wooster High.

Mia needed to find Chris and Pam's address in case she wanted to get a hold of them. She asked David and Sharon if they had any suggestions. Sharon immediately got into her car and drove the three miles to the office of Dickson Realty, where she worked as a realtor. There she could access names and addresses of Washoe County Property owners. A few minutes later David and Sharon called with the address—and a word of caution. They suggested that Mia take a deep breath, think over her incredible discovery, and then thoroughly consider the best course of action before acting.

"Don't move too fast," David suggested.

They proposed going out to dinner the following week to review Mia's options. They all agreed to keep the entire matter private, for there was no telling how the news would affect Pam and Chris, their families, and their lives. Mia had waited 33 years to learn her life's history; her in-laws thought she could wait a week longer, but they were kidding themselves.

Now that Mia had the address, Andy suggested driving by her birth parents' home, which was in Hidden Valley, a golf community a few miles east of downtown.

"No, I'd be too nervous," Mia said.

Andy's car license plate was in support of UNR and read "Quinn." Mia didn't want to chance recognition by Pam or Chris. Mia's license plate said "Mama Mia," so her car was definitely out. Mia had identified her birth parents less than three hours ago, and now she was becoming paranoid. What if Pam recognized Mia from Name Droppers? Mia didn't want to chance it; better to stay put. Then she pondered phoning them and immediately hanging up, just to see if they were in town. A high school move, to say the least, Mia thought. She chickened out. And a good thing too, since she later learned they had Caller ID.

That evening when she and Andy went to bed, Mia couldn't fall asleep. The night dragged on. She played the "what if" game in her mind almost until dawn. The next morning she realized how physically and mentally exhausted she was from crying. Years of pent-up emotions were pouring out of her in the form of laughter and tears. Her eyes were puffy and red from sobbing, and her nose was stuffy. She couldn't find the tissues fast enough. Her life had shifted so dramatically during the last 24 hours. Mia now saw the inescapable connection between her past and the present. There was no turning back. She felt as if she was on fast forward.

Her thoughts drifted to Pam. Mia remembered having a conversation with her once in the parking lot just outside Name Droppers. Mia was pregnant with Emmy at the time, and they discussed what it was like to have your first child. They stood there talking, never realizing that Mia was Pam's firstborn, pregnant with Pam's first grandchild. Mia couldn't fathom the fact she had known this woman and had spoken with her so many times. Pam often came into Name Droppers to buy gifts and get ideas for the first grade class she taught at Veterans Memorial Elementary School. As Mia recalled her visits with Pam throughout the years, she thought Pam had mentioned a son and daughter, but she couldn't remember for sure. Most of all, Mia pictured her birth mother's face over and over as she browsed the store softly humming to herself. Humming was an act Mia associated with a contented person. Mia smiled to herself at the idea that Pam appeared to be happy.

Something deep inside Mia kept her moving ahead. Now that she knew who her birth mother was, she couldn't wait any longer. She decided right then and there to find Pam and tell her she was her daughter. The desire was overwhelming—Mia couldn't wait another day, let alone another week.

Meanwhile, Emmy and Gilly were in the kitchen, hungry and ready for breakfast. It suddenly hit Mia: What if someone came into their life and turned it upside down? She looked at the girls and wondered how they would feel. She also considered their "right to know," and how this factor would weigh in the balance of her decision to tell Pam.

Mia suddenly became frightened. What will Pam and Chris think of me? How will they react? she thought. Since she was a little girl of seven, she thought her birth parents were "out there" missing her, loving her, and it would be the best day of their lives when they found her. Somehow, she always thought of her birth parents as being together, married. Now she had discovered it was so. And yet, what if they rejected her? What if they pretended she never existed? What if, what if, what if?

Mia's emotions were high as another thought hit her: What if Pam and Chris were to say to her, "We are sorry, Mia, but we put that part of our lives behind us many years ago and moved on, and so should you. You've had a good life and so have we. Now go away."

While the girls ate breakfast, Mia reflected about how supportive Andy, David, and Sharon had been. No one ever told her not to proceed with her investigation; they knew it meant too much to her. She knew this was her decision and that it scared her. She needed their support now more than ever.

Wounds from her mom Eileen's death were fresh in her mind. Today would have been Eileen's birthday, and though she and Mia's dad were gone, Mia still felt guilty, as if she was betraying them by reaching out to her birth parents. There were other emotions: the latent anger that adopted children sometimes experience, coupled with their deeply ingrained feeling of rejection. Mia was more vulnerable than ever. Andy asked her if she was prepared for any unpleasant developments that might surface. Mia prayed to her mom, asking for guidance. Perhaps this was a gift from her mom to Mia. Could it be that, instead of Mia giving a gift to her mom as she always had on her mom's birthday, her mom was giving the gift of discovery of her birth mother. Mia digested this thought as she went about dressing for work and getting the girls off to school.

The day dragged by, and Mia's thoughts weren't on either her store or her customers, but her mind was on the recurring doubts she had during the sleepless night before. Thank goodness I have such a supportive and understanding staff, Mia thought. They realize something is up, but have the good manners not to pry.

The Letter

Most people grow up aware of their biological history and knowing that they belong to some family. It may have been a good or bad relationship, but it was a base from which to grow. An adopted person has to grow without having a base. The longing to find one's roots varies from person to person. In Mia's case, she wanted to feel complete, like the feeling of closure you would get when completing a circle. It was of paramount importance to her.

Mia's workday was finally over. She drove home and fixed dinner, all the while trying to collect her thoughts and emotions. She pondered her feelings as she prepared to contact her birth parents. Mia had finally formulated a plan.

After they finished dinner, Mia said to Andy, "I've got to do this. I thought it over all night and decided a letter would be the best course of action."

A letter seemed to be the perfect solution. It would give Pam and Chris the privacy in which to react to the stunning news, and it would relieve Mia of what seemed the impossible task of making a coherent phone call. It would also spare her the vulnerability of just showing up on their doorstep unannounced, which, no matter how desperate she felt, she could never have done.

Mia began writing at the dining room table on sheets of red lined stationery. Every now and then she'd take a break to play with the girls or give them their baths. Then Andy kept them busy playing games while Mia got back to her writing. After tucking Emmy and Gilly into bed and saying prayers with them, Mia returned to the letter. Andy said goodnight around ten o'clock and wished Mia well. She stayed up late into the night, obsessed with communicating all of her feelings into a perfect letter— the most important letter of her life.

Finally the letter was finished. Mia read it again and again.

Feb. 26, 1999

Dear Pam and Chris:

There is no subtle way to begin this letter. Deep down I am hoping that you may have hoped one day I would contact you. I can't predict how this letter will affect you—whether I am an issue better left in the past or a door that might lead to the future.

I want you to know that I have discussed my recent and unexpected discovery of both of you only with my husband and my in-laws. I hold sincere respect for your privacy, as well as my own. I have thought long and hard about the "proper" way to contact you. Whether through opening files in court, a social worker, a mutual friend or a phone call, there seems no simple way. I decided that this should be between the both of you and me, and didn't want to involve any outsiders.

There have only been two other instances when I have felt such trepidation and emotion involved in writing a letter; unfortunately they were preparing testimonials for the funerals of both of my parents. It is an awesome task to express a lifetime of feelings in one letter.

I was born Toni Marie on November 11, 1965, in San Francisco, California. I was adopted through Family Agency here in Reno, Nevada, by a wonderful and loving family. Until recently I knew nothing about you other than your ethnic background. The fact that you lived in Reno and were both 18 at the time of my birth was only recently revealed.

*I have thought of you throughout my entire life—
but insecurities were always outweighed by the fact you
chose to give me life during a time of strict religious,
social and familial pressures, rather than choosing
the obvious alternative. I only recently decided to look
into my background. Upon learning your names, I
couldn't believe that you were eventually married and
was stunned to realize that I have seen and spoken
with you, Pam, several times. I could never explain the
impression you always left on me.*

*Your family name is very familiar to me, as mine
will probably be to you. It is not with a desire to be
claimed or named that I write to you. I have no idea
whether or not you know of my existence or whereabouts. It is purely from the heart that I contact both
of you. I have experienced the feelings of carrying and
giving birth to a child and the drastic effect it has on
your life. I have two daughters of my own—and so often
look at them and wonder what genetic traits are mine,
my husband's, and now yours.*

*I have experienced a multitude of emotions now
that I actually know who you are. I can now put a
face on an image that I have dreamed of for many,
many years. I will never be able to go backwards and
"unlearn" the reality of who you are, but I respect the*

fact that your feelings may not be mutual or even possible.

I have had a very happy, loved life and I feel over-whelmed with the vulnerability of this whole situation, confused about my expectations and the possible outcome.

The thought of a relationship between the three of us is indescribable, as is the possibility that you may have had other children that would be related to me, as well.

I'm unsure about what I should do next. I've read this letter a hundred times—I don't know if it was the right thing to do, writing to you—I just know I really needed to do it. I'm putting myself in your hands (once again).

Very truly yours,

Mia Brophy Quinn

Mia got into bed, but couldn't fall asleep. She tossed and turned and tried not to wake Andy. At around 2 o'clock she threw on her robe, went to the dining room, and read the letter for what seemed the hundredth time. What was it about 2 a.m.? That seemed to be the time to stress over the day's problems, all of which appeared to be huge at that early-morning hour.

Mia knew this letter would be her one and only opportunity. She might hear from Pam and Chris, she might not. But even if they never responded, she wanted them to know exactly how she, their daughter, felt. A few hours later she finally climbed back into bed. Then something else hit her. Pictures, she thought. She must include pictures with her letter. She would start looking for them first thing after breakfast. With that brilliant idea, Mia finally drifted off to sleep.

Early that Saturday morning Mia rummaged through albums and a box of old pictures she had saved from her mom's family collection. She pulled out a chronological selection, snapshots of herself as a baby, a toddler, in first through fifth grades, in high school, and on her honeymoon. Usually Mia got side-tracked when she started looking at old family photos, but this time she stayed on track. She taught scrap booking at her shop, and knew the importance of photographs in family record keeping. She placed the snapshots in the envelope, along with the letter and added her contact information to the last page.

Meanwhile, Andy called David and Sharon. "You guys are not going to believe what she's doing," he said. "She's written Pam and Chris a letter and she's going to mail it."

Ten minutes, later David and Sharon were at the front door ringing the bell. Andy let them in and showed them Mia's letter. As they read the heartfelt pages, tears welled up in their eyes.

"An excellent letter, Mia," David said with a warm smile.

Sharon could not speak. Her eyes glistened as she fought back the urge to cry after reading the heart-wrenching pages.

David and Sharon once again suggested going out to dinner the following Friday to discuss Mia's plan before she mailed the letter. A whole week away, Mia thought. David and Sharon were concerned for Pam's and Chris's privacy, and what this sudden, unexpected news might do to their family. But Mia's respect for their cautious opinion was overridden by her explosive feelings about her newfound discovery. She thanked them for their concern, but made no promises.

After Sharon and David left, Mia sealed the letter and photographs inside the envelope. She added extra postage for the weight of the pictures to ensure the package would arrive without delay. Then she placed the letter on the entry hall table. Could she really wait a week to mail it?

Later that morning Mia and Andy got Emmy and her gear ready for softball practice. As they headed for the car, Mia spied their letter carrier driving around the cul-de-sac delivering mail. On an impulse she ran back inside, grabbed the envelope off the hall table, and handed it to him as he approached the house. So much for cautious advice and clear thinking, Mia thought ruefully.

Mia knew she had made a spontaneous move—one only a frustrated adopted person could fully appreciate or understand. The excitement within her was similar to that of a child's on Christmas Eve waiting for Santa. Had she been good enough for him to fill her stocking and leave her some presents? The eternal optimist, Mia was hoping for the best.

Andy gave Mia an incredulous look as she got into the car. She was petrified, but she had to put her life completely together, for better or worse. Mia was aware the letter wouldn't be delivered until Monday. She stared out the car window, lost in thought and anticipation as they drove off to practice.

As Mia and her siblings were growing up, Mia's mom always had the family working on puzzles. Occasionally they would get close to the end, only to discover that several pieces were missing. It was not, nor would it ever be, complete. That's how she felt about her life, but the discovery of this new adoptive history was the missing piece. Mia hoped her life was finally coming together. She managed to get through the emotion-filled weekend by working around softball games and a dinner party. On Sunday night she began anticipating what might happen on Monday when the letter arrived at Pam's and Chris's home.

On Monday morning Mia jumped out of bed with alarm. "This could be the day Pam and Chris receive my letter!" she said to Andy. She suddenly found herself fear-stricken. What had she done? "We need to go over to their house and get the letter back after the mail is delivered."

Mia wanted Andy to drive over to Hidden Valley and stake out their mailbox. She was adamant.

Laughing in amazement, Andy said, "Mia, don't you know it's a federal offense to mess around with mail in someone else's mailbox?"

"Yes, I know. No, no, no...never mind," she stammered. "I want them to have it." She sounded like she had slipped into panic mode again.

Many scenarios had rushed through her mind over the weekend. What if Chris and Pam were wintering in Arizona, and wouldn't get the letter for a month or so? How would she know when they received it? David and Sharon had planned to suggest that Mia send the letter by registered mail so that she would get a confirmation of receipt, but it was too late. Oh, well, Mia thought. Saturday through Monday proved to be the longest three days of her life.

Monday went by...nothing! On Tuesday Mia went to work at the shop. The morning dragged by with no word from either Pam or Chris. Mia helped set up a new display for St. Patrick's Day. The arrival of colorful spring merchandise was always a favorite with the customers after the cold winter months, and lifted Mia's spirits. Mia spent time working on the store's books, but her concentration kept slipping.

Late that afternoon Mia left to run a few errands. When she returned, her manager told her a man had come into the store looking for her. Since she wasn't around, he left his business card. Mia raced over to the cash register where it had been placed for safekeeping. She reached for the card. It read: Chris Anastassatos, Human Resource Director, State of Nevada.

Mia's hand shook and her mouth was suddenly so dry it was difficult to swallow. She turned the card over and read: *Dear Mia, We got your letter, want to meet you very much. Love, Chris. Please call.*

After reading the card, Mia felt both jubilation and relief. She could hardly wait to talk with him. Her first phone call was to Andy. He was happy for her and couldn't wait to hear more. Mia was dazed and excited. Could it be? Was she finally going to get the chance to meet her birth parents?

During this time things were happening with Pam and Chris that Mia had no way of knowing about. They had been married four years after Mia was born and had two daughters, Kim and Kerrie. Now plans were being made for Kim's upcoming April marriage. Mia's letter did in fact arrive on Monday, but because of all the commotion concerning the upcoming event, Monday's mail and her letter were overlooked until late in the evening. Chris finally got around to opening the mail after Pam had gone to bed.

When Chris opened the letter, he thought the pictures inside were old photos of Pam, sent by a relative. Her mother had died in 1995. He figured someone in the family had found pictures and wanted Pam to have them. That's how much alike Mia and Pam looked as children. They had been receiving many cards and gifts, with the wedding just around the corner. Figuring this was yet another, he placed Mia's pictures and letter aside to read later after he opened the rest of the mail. After sorting through the large stack, he reached for Mia's letter again.

Chris could hardly breathe as he read a most beautiful letter from a daughter he thought he would never see. For all he knew, Mia could be dead. After all,

33 years had passed. After reading the letter many times over, Chris stared at the pictures of a little girl and her family, and of two granddaughters he never knew existed. Tears ran down his face as he read the pages again and again. Mia lived right here in Reno the whole time! His first reaction was to drive over to her home, take her in his arms and tell her how much he loved her.

He wanted to call Mia that night, but it was eleven-thirty. He refolded the pages and along with the photos, slipped them back into the envelope. Quietly he placed it in his dresser drawer, and crawled into bed without waking Pam. He needed to check things out first before he shared the letter with her.

Chris decided to stop by Name Droppers after his Lutheran Church meeting late on Tuesday afternoon. He walked into the shop and strolled around the store searching for Mia, until Carol asked if she could help him.

"I'm looking for Mia," he said.

Carol told him Mia was out running errands. He took a business card out of his pocket, wrote a note on the back, then handed the card to Carol and left the store.

When Chris got home that evening, he asked Pam to join him in their bedroom. He had something important to discuss. They had been going over photos and family memorabilia, so it was a good time to show her Mia's letter.

"I have something I want you to read," he said, handing the letter to Pam.

Pam glanced at the signature and said, "I know Mia. Why is she sending us this letter?"

Chris was speechless. How could this be? "You know Mia?" he stammered.

Pam calmly read the two-page letter. She looked over the photos and related to her husband that, amazingly, she knew Mia from shopping at Name Droppers. "In fact, I stood in the parking lot with Mia when she was pregnant and we discussed what it was like to have your first baby," she told Chris with disbelief in her voice. It was the same thought Mia had immediately after discovering Pam's identity.

Pam and Chris decided not to say anything to their daughters until after the wedding. "I don't know when I will tell Kim and Kerrie," Pam told Chris emphatically, "but I want to see Mia right away."

From home on Wednesday morning, Mia decided to call Chris at his office in Carson City. The store would be busy. She wasn't sure how much privacy she would have, nor how long the phone call would be. It was nine-thirty. Taking a deep breath she dialed the number.

"Chris, this is Mia," she said when Chris answered the call.

As soon as Chris heard Mia's voice he got up and shut his office door. His phone always rang, but on this day God held all the calls so he could get to know his daughter. "Mia!" Chris said. "I never thought we would find you. I love children and people and this feeling is so wonderful—a blessing from God, allowing us to meet our daughter. The idea of finding you never left my mind, but I thought you were adopted by people living in California. I hoped your adopted family would one day share the information with you. I would never have interrupted the adoptive parents and family unless they wanted to open the door."

A weight seemed to lift from Mia's shoulders as she heard her birth father's welcoming voice. She was excited to be talking with him and found she could breathe easier. Just suddenly knowing that her father cared for her was an amazing realization. She didn't know what she expected, but he was open and genuinely happy to talk to her. There was no anger in his voice only pure joy and excitement.

"Once I found about you and Pam living here in Reno, I knew I just had to get in touch," Mia said. "I know Pam from Name Droppers, but I never thought she was my mother! I really had no way of knowing."

Mia took in every word Chris said, hoping to remember it all. What a kind, gentle man she thought. She was amazed by the fact that he actually *wanted* to discuss her birth and adoption. Tears of joy kept flooding her eyes and she couldn't wait to talk with Pam. Would Pam feel similar emotions?

Later that same morning, Pam came into Mia's shop. Not seeing Mia at the register, she asked the clerk where Mia was. Pam was directed to Mia's office just off the room where she sold scrapbook supplies. Pam walked through the French doors and across the room with a photo in her hand. Mia looked up from her desk and saw Pam smiling as she came toward her.

This is Pam, my birth mother! Mia thought, hardly believing her eyes. This is really happening to me, after all these years of wishing and hoping. My biological mother and I are together for the second time in our lives as mother and daughter first at my birth in the San Francisco hospital and now in my shop!

Pam handed Mia the photo and said in a soft voice, "Mia, I am your mom and here is your birth family."

Mia's heart didn't just skip a beat; it pounded so hard she thought it would burst when she realized that

Pam was actually there to see her. Then Mia started worrying. I hope she isn't upset with me, she thought. What should I say to her? Would she be as easy to talk with as Chris?

Pam stood there, very matter-of-factly and not a bit shy or embarrassed. Mia hadn't known what to expect, but here she was talking with her birth mother!

After a reunion with lots of smiles, tears, kisses, and hugs, Mia and Pam needed some privacy and a quiet place to talk. Mia's knees felt weak and she needed to sit down. She had so many questions— questions she had kept locked up inside her for what seemed like a lifetime.

A Love Story

MIA AND PAM MADE their way from the shop to the Country Garden Restaurant at Arlington Gardens a few stores away inside the small, enclosed mall. The restaurant was busy as usual, filled with business people, neighbors and ladies who lunch. Mia and Pam walked through the indoor patio with its old worn brick floors and decorative iron railing into the main dining area. They were shown to a table for two in front of glass doors that opened onto a path leading to the nursery.

As they drew up their chairs, Mia looked at Pam. Here is my birth mother, sitting across from me, she thought. In a way she felt detached, as though she was watching two strangers talking. Excitement and nerves were having a field day with her emotions. The server arrived and they both agreed to order a hot pot of spiced tea.

Even though Mia had just gotten off the phone with Chris, she had many questions and wanted to hear all the details Pam was willing to share. First and foremost was: How did I end up being born in San Francisco? Soon after their tea arrived, Pam related the story—the love story she shared with Chris.

Pam said that Angelo was Chris's Greek middle name, the name he was baptized with. His work friends at the Air National Guard and his Nevada State office called him Chris, but old friends and, especially, family members called him Angelo.

Angelo is what I will call him from this moment on, Mia thought.

As Pam poured them both a cup of the steaming hot, fragrant tea, she took a deep breath and started her story. "Our first encounter began in the 9th grade at Traner Middle School. We were attracted to each other, and in no time Angelo asked me to go steady. The year went by quickly and we could feel romance in the air."

"I started 10th grade at Reno High, but Angelo was disappointed to learn that his family home was rezoned for Wooster High, the new school across town near the airport. After all, four of his brothers and two of his three sisters had attended Reno High. He would be enrolling at Wooster and he was disappointed he couldn't carry on the family tradition."

"We spent as much time together as we could, attending school dances and sporting events. We continued dating, and by our senior year realized we had been in love with each other for a long time. When I told Angelo that I had become pregnant, he was speechless. The unthinkable had happened. What were we going to do?"

Pam sipped her tea, and then continued, "Angelo turned to his older brother, Spiros, for help. Spiros was 28, a college graduate who had married his sweetheart, Popi. Spiros and Popi talked about keeping the baby and raising it as their own, but decided a child's presence would be difficult to explain to their parents. Greek families are very close-knit, proud, and strict. Angelo's elderly parents would never have understood our situation. Although his father and mother had lived in the States for years, they were entrenched in Greek customs and family traditions. They would never learn of our baby. In fact, Angelo's mother didn't learn to speak English even though she lived in Reno for over 50 years. Greek family ways forbid children from even starting to date until they reach 18, so Angelo was already in hot water."

"My mother and I wanted to raise you, Mia, but it would have been difficult to explain to our family, as well. We both worked and I would soon be starting college. My mother and grandmother were always so supportive; I don't know how I would have gotten through my pregnancy without them."

"During the spring semester of our last year in high school, Spiros and his sister Alex were very intent on making arrangements and finding the money to pay the hospital fees for my stay in San Francisco. Only a few family members knew what was going on between Angelo and me."

Mia listened in utter silence as she tried to absorb every word she was hearing.

"I would often get off work to attend Angelo's baseball games at Wooster High, but this time it was different. Wooster had advanced to the AAA State Championships and would be playing at the semi-pro Moana Ball Park. I didn't want him to know I was standing on the street outside the fence watching him through the wooden slats. He was embarrassed and had been avoiding me; I was sad and hurt. After all, I was carrying our child and he didn't seem to care. It took me several unhappy months to get over his actions, but by August, we had reconciled."

"My father never learned of the pregnancy. My dad was told I was being sent to San Francisco for a two-month training class for St. Mary's Hospital, where I worked part-time as a medical records clerk."

At that moment Mia wondered if Pam and John, Mia's adopted dad, had ever met at St. Mary's. They both worked at the hospital at the same time! Maybe—just maybe—he knew of Pam's pregnancy. Mia guessed she would never know.

"In September I got on a bus with just my suitcase and headed for the Bay Area. We had both graduated in June, and now I was going to spend the rest of my pregnancy with strangers. The family I lived with in San Rafael was pleasant and understanding, for they had taken in other pregnant girls over the years. In return for room and board, I took care of their young son, Jack. Angelo wrote to me several times during my stay, giving his love, support, and encouragement, but nonetheless I felt alone and frightened in a strange city without my family around to help and comfort me. I longed for a friend to talk to."

Pam paused while Mia picked up the teapot and refilled their cups. Mia often had tears in her eyes as she listened intently to Pam's story. Mia didn't have to ask many questions, because the whole adoption story just poured out of Pam.

"Angelo was sent by the Air National Guard to a Midwest basic training camp in August. He didn't return to Reno until December. During those last few weeks in October, I moved to the expectant mothers' dorm at Saint Elizabeth's Children's Hospital to wait for the delivery. Toni Marie, the name Angelo and I decided to call you, was born on November 11, 1965. We both agreed the best thing was to put you up for adoption. We felt this would give you the opportunity for a good and complete life."

"For the two weeks after your birth, the nurses would bring you into my room for me to hold. I looked down at your tiny sweet face and knew we could never be together. They took a Polaroid snapshot of you and gave me the picture. My stay at the hospital came to an abrupt end when a nurse took you out of my arms for the last time and carried you down the hall to the adoption agency."

Mia had learned just that morning during her phone conversation with Angelo that his brother Spiros had visited Pam in the hospital. As the senior male voice of the Anastassatos family, he felt it important to visit Pam and lend his family's support, especially since Angelo was away on military duty and couldn't see Pam or the baby.

Pam went on, "Angelo and I had conceived you in love, but circumstances kept us apart. Two weeks after your birth, I took my first ever plane trip back to Reno, and the next chapter of my life as a University of Nevada student began."

Mia just sat there and stared. Pam told her story methodically and with poise. Even her emotions seemed controlled. What an incredible story she had just shared! They each took a drink of tea and continued their conversation of discovery.

"What had become of our adopted baby girl, Toni Marie?" Pam said. "We wondered if you were in San Francisco or in some other part of the country. The only thing I had to show Angelo when I got home was the small black and white Polaroid. We keep it hidden away in a small box in my nightstand." Pam picked up her teacup and gazed out the French doors toward the nursery.

The fact that Mia had been taken to Reno and adopted by John and Eileen Brophy was nothing short of a miracle.

"I enrolled in college for the spring semester and started working at Sears," Pam continued. "I had always loved children and decided to become an elementary school teacher. Angelo began university classes at the same time. We started dating again and three-and-a-half years later, I graduated with a teaching degree. In 1968, the Pueblo Incident occurred in the waters off North Korea and Air National Guard members were called to active duty. Angelo left college and served 16 months with the Guard in Kansas. He took a few classes at Wichita State, which applied to his university requirements.

"After returning to Reno, Angelo decided he liked working at the Guard. He would stay on full-time and finish his college education in his off hours. Angelo went to night classes and completed his requirements for a degree. It took him over 20 years from the time he entered UNR until he graduated. I was so proud of him for finishing his studies," Pam finished happily with a warm smile.

What a story! Mia thought. Her first response was to rush home and share it with Andy, but she was physically and emotionally overwhelmed. She had been concentrating intently so as not to miss a word. She wished she had taken a tape recorder or dashed down some notes, but she knew that would have appeared insensitive.

Pam and Mia were exhausted after three hours of conversation and several pots of tea. Strangely, during their teatime in the restaurant not one person interrupted them. Mia knew all the women who worked at

Arlington Gardens Mall and many of its customers; perhaps people could see how important the conversation was between these two women.

Though tired, Mia was eager to learn more. She had 33 years of catching up to do with her newfound family, but she knew it wouldn't all happen in one afternoon. Mia and Pam said their goodbyes in the parking lot and walked toward their cars. Then Pam suddenly turned to Mia and said softly, "Mia, I can't deal with this right now. I'm busy with Kim's wedding."

Mia's spirits fell. She had a hard time catching her breath. At the restaurant, Pam had been pleasant, but somewhat guarded. This became clear to Mia, now that the excitement of the meeting was waning. She didn't know what she had anticipated, but it was clear that Pam was protecting her family. It suddenly dawned on Mia that she was an intruder. In Pam's place, Mia might have done the same thing. Their first moments together were wonderful, yet distressing. It was bittersweet. Mia knew she had to give Pam time to digest the news. She was expecting too much too soon. After all, Mia had thrust this information at Pam and Angelo less than a week ago, and Pam had come to see her as soon as Angelo told her about the letter. It was a promising start.

Mia felt a crushing pain in her heart. Andy warned me, she reflected. Then she began to strengthen. She would not let her emotions get the better of her. She thanked Pam and hugged her warmly, then mother and daughter parted ways.

As she looked back on their meeting, Mia thought the most astonishing thing was that Pam and Angelo had been together since the 9th grade. Their love had been tested through separation, the pregnancy, and Mia's birth. They came from passionate families, and these strong upbringings helped to form their characters. They never gave up. They found a way to always be together. Their wedding occurred four years after Mia was born, in August of 1969. Pam then began her teaching career, while Angelo continued to work for the Air National Guard.

The next two months would be hectic for Pam, Angelo, Kim, and Kerrie. The wedding was near and the whole family was involved in the coming events. Although Mia had found her birth parents, she knew she was still a secret to their daughters. And as Mia got on with the responsibilities of her own daily life, she wondered what the future would bring.

The Monday night after the revelation, Angelo went to Mia and Andy's home to show them his huge photo album of Greece. This was Mia's first opportunity to meet Angelo in person, so Andy decided to take Gilly and Emmy out to dinner to give them time alone together. Soon after they left, Angelo walked up to the front porch and rang the bell. Mia was standing just inside the entry. She opened the door immediately, wearing a big grin on her face. Angelo was also smiling, and as he came into the house, he gave Mia a warm hug. The Greeks really know how to hug! Mia thought happily.

Mia's world stood still. Her birth father was *really* in her home—hugging her! She was in his arms for the first time. She had tears of joy in her eyes, and so did he. Mia had dreamed of this moment, but didn't dare let herself ever think it would come true. Angelo was 51 the first time Mia saw him. He was of average height and very solid. His eyes seemed to twinkle as he talked, and when he smiled his cheeks puffed out. With extra padding, he would have made the perfect department store Santa.

Mia led him into the family room, where Andy had a cozy fire going. It was the perfect setting for a serene evening. Mia immediately started to relax, just being in Angelo's presence. Belle, the family's blond cocker spaniel, was outside the French patio doors pleading to come inside. Angelo told Mia he also had a cocker spaniel, one of their many similarities.

"Mia," he said, "I want to make sure you are not upset with Pam, because she always wanted to keep you. It was me and my family who resisted. I want you to direct any harsh feelings toward me, not Pam."

Mia replied, "Angelo, I am just now beginning to learn what happened concerning my adoption. I realize my birth must have affected your two families enormously."

Angelo continued, "There are so many things I want to tell you, but first I want to know all about you."

Over the next two hours, Mia told him stories of her early childhood and family history. She shared her memories of school, meeting Andy, their marriage, and the births of Emmy and Gillian. Mia described the incredible summer vacations to their family owned island in Canada. She explained the decision and thrill of buying Name Droppers. She felt so at ease talking with Angelo. Their time together melted away like the assortment of candles burning across the mantle above the fireplace.

At the same time, back at Angelo's home, Kim and Kerrie were worried because it was not like their dad to be away so long. "Where has he gone, and why is he so late?" they both continued to ask Pam, who kept repeating that he was visiting friends who were interested in an upcoming trip to Greece.

A few hours later, Andy returned home, carrying a sleeping child draped over each shoulder. Emmy and Gilly had fallen asleep in the car on the way back from dinner. Careful not to interrupt Mia and Angelo, he put the girls to bed, then joined Mia in the family room to meet Angelo. The moment Andy walked in the room he said, "I can't believe how much you two look alike. Anyone can see the resemblance between father and daughter. It's in your face, especially in your eyes and your smiles."

Angelo and Andy are both very charismatic individuals and immediately took a liking to each other. Mia and Angelo brought Andy up-to-date on their discussion, and then proceeded to look through the photo album. The trio sat on the sofa, with Angelo in the middle and the album on his lap. Mia and Andy got a complete photo tour of Greece, including Angelo's beautiful family island of Kefalonia, which lies in the Ionian Sea west of Athens. Angelo was animated and enthusiastic when he spoke. You couldn't help but like him.

"It's so gorgeous, we can hardly wait to go there someday," Mia and Andy told him.

Angelo showed them pictures of his ancestral home and the relatives who were still living on the island. They saw photos of his brothers and sisters. The snapshots of the sea, taken from their house high upon the hillside, were breathtaking and picturesque. Scenes of orchards, vineyards, and small villages were so perfect they looked like photos from a travel book. Angelo shared with them the astounding story of how his family escaped from Greece and came to America when he was just a few months old. He gave other fascinating accounts about his ancestors in Greece. As he spoke, it occurred to Mia that this colorful history was now part of her family background; these stories would become her stories. Yes, she thought, I really do have a history! Listening to Angelo recall the many anecdotes about the lives of his brothers and sisters made her feel like she belonged to this remarkable family.

As the evening flew by, Andy stoked the fire and added a few more logs while Angelo pulled out another set of pictures he wanted them to see. They were pictures of Kim and Kerrie, Mia's real blood sisters. They smiled up at Mia from the album pages. Andy could tell how excited she was to see them. She barely contained her enthusiasm as she looked at their photos. Mia didn't recall ever meeting them or seeing them in her shop.

Hours later, the trio realized it was impossible to relate such vast amounts of history in so little time. They agreed they would have a lifetime to share past family events and make new stories of their own. Just after midnight, as Angelo was preparing to leave, Mia and Andy asked him if he would like to peek in on the children. They walked down the hallway to the girls' bedrooms and slowly opened their doors. Angelo looked at Emmy, then at Gilly, sleeping in their beds. He smiled as he saw his two granddaughters for the very first time. Then, with another big hug, Angelo was on his way.

Andy and Mia were so energized, they couldn't go to bed. They both had to work the next day and needed time to let the adrenaline settle down before even attempting to call it a night. They went back into the family room, let Belle inside, and collapsed on the sofa. Mia filled Andy in on more of the details she and Angelo had discussed while he and the girls were at dinner. Andy and Mia agreed that Angelo was easy-going and fun to be with. He had been open and enthusiastic about all of his history with Pam and the family.

One thing that impressed Mia about meeting both Angelo and Pam was their honesty in relating their difficult experience from long ago. She realized that they had had time to get over the stigma. They were both well-adjusted young people who loved each other and who had worked through the complicated issue of Mia's birth.

Mia and Andy were both talked out and decided to call it a night. As Mia fell asleep, she thought over her visit with Angelo. She couldn't have imagined a nicer, friendlier person. She could see definite personality differences between Angelo and her dad John, yet at the same time parallels in both. Her dad was formal in manner and dress, with a deliberate style in the way he spoke. She remembered him as a loving and giving person, but with an aristocratic, methodical approach to life. He enjoyed telling stories and sharing family history in the same way Angelo did. While Angelo was easy going and casual in his manner, he possessed the same charismatic style as Mia's dad. She felt fortunate to have been raised by her dad, and to now have her birth father, Angelo, in her life. She wondered what the two men would have thought of each other had they ever met.

A few weeks after their evening with Angelo, he called and asked if he and Pam could come over for a visit.

"Of course," Mia said enthusiastically. "I'm anxious for Andy to meet Pam."

Mia arranged for their baby sitter, Natalina, to take the girls to dinner. Andy and Mia hadn't told the children about Pam and Angelo. They were waiting for the right opportunity, just as Pam and Angelo were waiting for the best time to tell Kim and Kerrie. Natalina was still getting the girls dressed when Pam and Angelo arrived. Mia introduced Andy to Pam, and they headed for the family room just as the girls came down the hallway. Mia wanted the girls to meet Pam and Angelo and said they were "friends of mommy's and daddy's." The girls were polite, smiled, and said hello. As Gilly turned to go out the door with Emmy and Natalina, she looked back at Angelo and said, "Goodbye, Grandpa."

Andy, Mia, Pam and Angelo all looked at one another, stunned. How did a three-year-old know this stranger was her grandpa?

The foursome enjoyed talking and sharing stories back and forth. Pam seemed more relaxed talking with Mia and Andy than she had at the first meeting in the restaurant. After returning from dinner, Emmy and Gilly came into the family room to visit with Pam and Angelo. Mia wondered what was going through her birth parents' minds at the sight of their two little granddaughters. It was a wonderful night. Everything had gone well. Now Mia anxiously awaited the day she would meet her sisters.

Mia had dear friendships that reached back to elementary school and college. One of her closest friends is Kelli Newman; the two were sorority sisters and shared many memories. When Mia told Kelli about her newfound family, Kelli was surprised and shocked that Mia actually decided to ask questions about the details of her adoption. Mia asked Kelli what she thought of the whole idea. Kelli encouraged her dear friend. "I would look for my birth parents and do everything I possibly could to find them," she said. "Mia, you must be so excited to know you have other relatives."

Angelo and Pam

Wedding Day, August 1969, Reno, NV

Unionville

Mia was overwhelmed by the events of the previous few months, so David and Sharon arranged some time away for both families to unwind. Kathy Quinn, Mia's sister-in-law, joined the group with her two children, Mike and Makena. It was the first weekend of April 1999.

They were headed for the Pioneer Garden Country Inn. It sat in a picturesque canyon in the Humboldt Range above Buena Vista Valley, a few hours east of Reno, down the road past Winnemucca. The historic two-story bed and breakfast was built in the 1860s as a small hotel for early pioneers who mined the canyons nearby, and was the perfect place to get away.

As the three-car caravan turned off the main road and headed up the canyon, they drove by a herd of sheep and their Basque sheepherders. Andy turned to the girls and said, "Take a look at those sheep with their shepherds and dogs. You don't see that very often."

They pulled over and watched the border collies run back and forth, keeping the herd in line.

The family rented the entire inn for a long weekend. The owners, a World War II fighter pilot and his wife, lived in the house next door. The inn included six bedrooms of various sizes, two baths, cozy sofas and chairs, a stone fireplace, a funky solarium and a warm, inviting study with book-lined walls. Just looking at the titles on the old book jackets was a step back in time. They cooked their meals on the wood-burning iron stove that was wedged into a corner of the large kitchen. They all brought enough food to last a month. Most of the cooking utensils were from the 1940s, and everyone took turns using them to prepare the meals. Old mixing bowls, cast iron pots, pans, and dishes lined the tall, glass-front cabinets. A long, worn harvest farm table ran down the middle of the room and could easily seat twelve.

Pam and Angelo had just visited with Mia and Andy a few nights before the trip, and Mia was so excited it was all she could talk about. Kimmy's wedding was still a few weeks away. Then Mia had to wait until Angelo and Pam decided when to tell Kimmy and Kerrie they had a long-lost sister. It was after Mia saw Kim's photos that she decided to call her Kimmy. It was the name her immediate family called her, and seemed to fit. She appeared upbeat and fun-loving in her pictures—somehow she just looked like a "Kimmy."

Friday night, as the women were fixing dinner, Kathy asked Mia, "Mia, have you thought about what your sisters might be like?"

Mia responded, laughing, "Yes, all the time. Pam said they are five and seven years younger than me. It will be great to be the older sister for a change. Just think, I was the baby in the Brophy family, and now I'm the oldest child in Pam and Angelo's family."

"Are you sure you've never seen them at the store? I thought you knew most of your customers," Kathy asked, while tearing the lettuce greens for their dinner salad.

"I thought so, too, but I guess I missed a few," Mia said, reaching to get the French bread out of the oven. "Maybe when I have a chance to meet my sisters and really look at them, I'll remember, but for now, I'm clueless. Pam mentioned that they shopped at the store, but I just don't recall seeing or speaking with either of them. Maybe they came by on my days off."

In the evenings they played poker, Monopoly, and watched old movies in the living room. A writing desk was close by, with a guest book that held entries from celebrities, politicians, and folks on holiday, all promising to return one day for a visit. Out the back door and down several steep wooden steps was a worn dirt path. It led to a shaded, secluded sitting area next to a stream lined with cottonwood and sycamore trees. Mia spent a few quiet moments there in one of the weathered Adirondack chairs, reminiscing about the past few weeks. The water was freezing, but the gurgling sound was soothing as she tried to recall, day by day, the amazing events unfolding in her life. She had discovered who her birth parents were and had talked with them several times. They had met Andy, Emmy, and Gilly. Dave and Sharon knew the family and many of their brothers and sisters from years ago. Questions about the past 33 years were being answered, and it was all more than Mia had hoped for. Her next encounter would be meeting Kimmy and Kerrie, and Mia began to wonder and worry all over again. Will they like me? Will I remember them from the store? Do we have mutual friends and know the same people? She thought about the question Kathy had asked. Why can't I remember them? Mia couldn't believe their paths had never crossed. The three of them, separately, had been involved with cheerleading.

They had attended many UNR events, both in and out of college. Mia couldn't wait to meet her sisters.

As she watched the girls playing with Andy across the lawn, her thoughts returned to the time just after Emmy was born. Mia would often look at her and think there was no chance she could ever give Emmy away or be apart from her. She found herself having the same thoughts after Gilly's birth. Just thinking about the idea of a baby being born and then being separated from its birth mother, was distressing.

She tried several times to read her book, but her thoughts kept drifting back to her first meeting with Pam. Mia was trying to put the conversation in order and remember all of the details to the many questions she had asked Pam. The more she remembered about their talk, the more she realized that the answers only led to more questions. Enough, she thought. All in good time. She walked over to the pasture where Emmy and Gilly were chasing a small herd of sheep and lambs near a small round wooden corral made of bent tree branches. The herd was agile and scattered across the field when they saw the giggling little girls heading their way.

Each evening as the sun descended behind the rugged mountains at the ridge of the canyon and dusk rolled around, the family kept a close eye on Gilly, as did the ugly-looking buzzards perched in the top of several ancient, half-dead cottonwood trees. She was just the right size for their nightly meal.

In the early morning hours, a small group of deer could be seen grazing on the dewy-laden meadow. Occasionally two or three distracted does would look back at their observers, then nonchalantly return to nibbling the wet grass. David and Andy spotted fresh paw prints from a mountain lion that cruised through the canyon each day prior to breakfast. The deer scattered as the hungry group traipsed down the path and through the quaint cottage garden on their way to the owner's home, where a huge country feast was waiting to be devoured.

Andy took the kids fishing in the pond a few times. They caught some small trout, which they fried on the old kitchen stove for dinner appetizers. Before dinner, Dave and Sharon gathered the grandchildren for walks up the canyon to look at the dilapidated cabins left over from a hundred years ago when men worked the mines. One of those prospectors was a young writer with the pen name of Mark Twain. He lived in the canyon for a short time, hoping to strike it rich. The air was still, and there was a wonderful calmness about the place, calmness they all tried to emulate.

After breakfast on Sunday, they packed up and said their goodbyes. It had been a restful weekend away from the telephones and work.

During the road trip back to Reno, Mia's thoughts returned to her sisters. When would Pam and Angelo speak to them, and what will Kimmy and Kerrie have to say?

Sisters

THERE WAS A SMALL wooden box in the bottom drawer of Pam's nightstand. Kimmy had been trying for years to secretly open it when no one was looking. She and Kerrie were dying to know what was hidden inside the mysterious wooden container. It wasn't heavy, and nothing inside seemed to move or make noise when it was jiggled.

Kimmy and Mark Welker had just enjoyed a fabulous Greek wedding a few weeks earlier and were living with Pam and Angelo until their new home was completed. Kerrie was also living with her folks while deciding on her career options. Pam and Angelo had bought their home in 1972, several years following their marriage, and it was large enough for all.

One afternoon shortly after the wedding, when everyone was at home, Angelo saw the girls coming down the hall and asked them to come into the master bedroom. Angelo and Pam had just finished a serious discussion concerning Mia's letter and they decided it was time to share the news with Kimmy and Kerrie. As the girls entered the room, Angelo closed the door. He said that he and Pam had something important to say, and motioned for them to sit down on the bed. Their parents looked very serious; Kerrie and Kimmy couldn't imagine what had happened.

Angelo took Mia's letter out of his pocket and gave it to his daughters. Kimmy read it aloud slowly, trying to comprehend its contents. Emotions welled up inside everyone. As she finished the letter, the sisters were overcome by feelings of protection for their family, excitement over the discovery of a long-lost sister, and bewilderment. What was going on? What had just happened to change their lives forever? Why weren't they ever told about an older sister? Their family was without secrets, or so they had thought.

Over the next tearful hour, Angelo and Pam explained the long story of the pregnancy, adoption, and how Mia came to live in Reno. They discussed the involvement of select family members who had arranged for Pam to be sent to San Francisco for Mia's birth, and how Pam had wanted to keep Mia. They went on to explain how and why the secret was kept from Pam's father and Angelo's parents.

Kimmy and Kerrie were totally amazed and slightly confused. Then Angelo reached for a stack of pictures on the dresser.

"These are pictures of your sister," he said. He showed them the childhood pictures Mia had included with the letter. The girls looked carefully at each photo of Mia.

Pam and Angelo still had the little wooden box that once held a picture of a newborn taken in a hospital in San Francisco. Every so often, either Pam or Angelo would open the box and look at the well-worn black and white photo of the little baby girl. Two years before Mia started her inquiry, they opened the tiny box and looked at the picture of their baby for the last time. Then they removed the small snapshot and destroyed it. They felt that if they kept the photo in the box much longer, Kimmy or someone else would find a way to peer inside. The image only brought sadness and reminded them of that early conflict between the families. What could be done? The child was part of an earlier time. It was best to forget it ever happened.

Pam and Angelo explained to Kimmy and Kerrie that the letter from Mia had arrived over two months before the wedding, but they decided to wait for the family's life to return to normal before telling them. Planning the wedding had been enjoyable, but time and energy consuming. Pam and Angelo needed a rest before tackling the next chapter in their lives. Not only would Kimmy and Kerrie have an enormous amount of questions, but so would family, friends, and, as they were to find out later, complete strangers.

After listening to her sister read the letter, seeing the photographs and hearing her parents telling their side of the story, Kerrie stood up, walked across the bedroom, opened the door, and went out into the hallway. She needed time to sort out what had just happened in her life. A sister she knew nothing about had just contacted her family. What did all this mean? Born in 1977, she discovered she was now the youngest of three sisters. She needed time to quietly arrange her thoughts concerning the earthshaking disclosure she had just heard.

Kimmy, Mia's gregarious, inquisitive sister, couldn't ask questions fast enough. She was born in 1974, and now realized she was the middle child. She didn't care. Kimmy asked where Mia had been and where she lived—she was so excited that she wanted to see her right away.

All those years growing up in the enormous Anastassatos family, Kimmy and Kerrie had never heard the family rumor about a baby being born to someone among them long ago. Sharon, Mia's mother-in-law, heard the rumor from her late friend, Marilyn Lewis Anastassatos, who was married to Angelo's brother, Jerry. Through the years that followed the adoption Angelo would hear about "sightings," as he referred to them, from someone in the family who knew of the adoption. He would sometimes see a woman the approximate age Mia would be and wondered if it might be his daughter from long ago. A few of his knowing brothers and sisters urged him to look for Mia, but he decided the subject was best left alone. After all, he thought, their baby was hopefully adopted and living in California.

All through their growing-up years, they had shopped at Name Droppers with Pam for gifts, papers, and cards. As they grew older and started driving, they visited the store, but didn't recall ever meeting Mia. They tried hard to remember her appearance, but couldn't place her face. They just had to know who she was and what she looked like.

The next day Kimmy and Kerrie started calling Name Droppers after store hours just to hear Mia's voice on the answering machine; but the voice they heard was one of the employees, not Mia's. They even drove over to Andy and Mia's home on Ayershire Court to see where they lived. Kimmy was relentless in her search—a super-sleuth.

Seeing her sisters for the first time was one of the happiest moments in Mia's life. They had arranged for a meeting with Mia early Thursday morning, just a few days after their discovery. Mia was beside herself with excitement. Would they accept her or would they just walk away and be upset for her encroachment into their family? Mia feared they might be protective of their parents and furious with her for daring to enter into their lives. Her "what ifs" were back in her thoughts, working overtime. Then the doorbell rang. Mia opened the door and there they were: Kimmy and Kerrie.

They all broke into huge smiles, and all three instantly realized how much they looked alike. Mia showed them through the kitchen and into the family room. There they spent the next ten hours getting to know one another. They talked about their early childhoods, schooling, church, likes and dislikes, Pam and Angelo, and the whole Anastassatos family, all 70 of them. Mia had always wanted a big family with cousins, aunts, and uncles. This was perfect, she thought—over the top! They all loved the Christmas holiday season, and shared their different traditions on celebrating. The list went on and on.

Their conversation became serious when they discussed Mia's adoption and the effect it had on their family those many years ago. Mia had had a few months to get used to the fact, but Kimmy and Kerrie had just learned about their older sister. They were three young women, trying to catch up on their entire life histories in one day.

They laughed over former boyfriends, dates they had been on, and parties they had attended. The sisters discovered that their hands and feet looked exactly the same. Their love of skiing and other outdoor activities was mutual. The three had been cheerleaders in school and were big fans of the athletic teams at the university. Shopping for the latest in clothing fashions and home décor were both favorites of the trio. Current events, movies, books, and travel were shared interests. They discussed their goals and ventures into the business world. Both of their families were active in the community with volunteer and church activities, so the sisters found they had many friends and acquaintances in common. Kimmy and Kerrie had been to Greece, and Mia was anxious to hear about their trip. Questions! They all had so many questions!

Later that morning, as the sisters chattered away, Mia's friend Tammy Ernst dropped by to say hello and to ask if Mia wanted to join her for a bit of shopping. When she knocked on the front door, Mia shouted for her to come in. Tammy walked into the family room, took one look at the three of them and said, "These are your sisters, aren't they?" She stayed for a while and listened in amazement to their nonstop conversation. Later, Andy came home from work and greeted them, with Emmy in tow. Emmy was shy but friendly as she met her new aunts. She seemed to sense they were very special.

The day passed by quickly as the sisters continued to get to know one another. Mia's sisters feared that because she was raised in a doctor's home, she might be aloof and fussy what they thought of as the quintessential "doctor's daughter." They were pleased to discover that Mia was pretty normal. Besides, with Kimmy and Kerrie around, Mia wouldn't have a chance to get a big head; they would just tell her to "get over it."

This first meeting was the beginning of many wonderful times together. They began to sneak away to Unionville to have girls' weekends. Sometimes they asked friends to join in the fun. They would laugh, gossip, cook, drink wine, and have an all around great party.

As word got out that Mia had found her birth family (thanks largely to sister Kimmy and Mia's in-laws sharing the story with friends), people would come to Name Droppers just to hear Mia's account. Friends and customers were amazed by the seemingly simple process of her spontaneous trip to the adoption agency turning into an amazing, life-changing event. Everyone Mia came in contact with was thrilled for her.

The Sisters
Kerrie, Kimmy and Mia

The Afghan

ONE OF THE FAMILY'S favorite moments in Mia's whole discovery process was her meeting with the senior member of the family, Aunt Sofia. Sofia lives in Reno with her husband Pierre. They have a lovely brick home on Skyline Boulevard, across the street from Mia's Uncle Spiros and Aunt Popi.

Mia and Andy were invited to meet Sophia and Pierre one afternoon shortly after Mia's discovery. When they walked up to her front door, it swung wide open in a rush. Aunt Sophia started crying the moment she saw Mia. She invited them in, gave Mia a warm hug, and then showed them to one of the sofas in the beautifully furnished formal living room. Refreshments and delicious Greek cookies were offered as she began to tell the story of her proud heritage.

Sofia recalled marvelous and dramatic incidents about the lives of her family, both here and in Greece.

She shared with them her father Christos's first trip to New York City in 1910, and how he was sent to Reno by his employer to work on the mail cars for the railroad. She was proud of his accomplishments becoming an American citizen, and his employment with R. Herz and Brothers Jewelers in Reno. Sophia recounted his heroics as he fought with the American Army in France during World War I and his eventual return to his beloved Greek island of Kefalonia, where he soon married and raised a family. She told heartwarming stories that would fill a book about her family's incredible and dangerous escape after World War II from the Greek Communists. Christos fled to America with his two oldest daughters and son and made his way back to Reno. There, they worked hard and earned the funds to send for his wife Irene and the remaining children, including baby Angelo.

The walls of Sofia's home were lined with countless photos recording the lives of her ancestors. As Aunt Sofia spoke about the family history that afternoon, she suddenly excused herself and said, "I need to get something in the next room." She walked slowly down her hallway and into one of the bedrooms. Mia and Andy could hear her open a closet door. A few minutes later, she returned to the living room carrying a folded afghan in her hands. She placed it in Mia's outstretched arms. She explained that her mother, Irene, had crocheted an afghan for each grandchild born into their family. She went on to say her mother had made an extra one, one to be given to a child that may be added to the family sometime in the future. Irene was not sure when the time would come, but she relied on Aunt Sofia to know the proper moment and person. Irene had told her, "You will know what to do with it someday."

Sophia's eyes filled with glimmering tears of happiness as she shared this story. Mia's tears tumbled down her face as her arms folded over the soft, beautiful afghan. At that moment Mia glanced at Andy, and his eyes were shining above his marvelous grin. What a wonderful confirmation! Mia finally felt that she truly belonged to this loving family—the family she had longed for all her life. This was really happening to her, and she relished every moment of this glorious afternoon, thanking God for her second beginning.

Quinn Children
Left to Right: Gilly, Jack and Emmy, 2004

No Longer A Puzzle

As THE YEARS PASS, the intertwining of Mia's two lives seems to be natural. Mia now finds herself at peace with who she is. The feelings she has regarding her new sisters are open, affectionate, and real, they all share an unconditional love. They are both honest and fun-loving with a casual grace—the same today as at their first meeting. Kimmy is talkative, enthusiastic, and selfless. Kerrie is thoughtful, giving, yet outspoken, with a no-nonsense personality. Their sisterhood has blended together like wet paint on watercolor paper.

Andy and Mia were sorry to have missed Kimmy's wedding ceremony. The reception was a large, formal, Greek-style celebration, held at the beautiful Lightning W (now Thunder Canyon) Country Club nestled next to mountains in Washoe Valley. But the wedding was only two months after Mia wrote her letter, and the family wasn't ready for explanations.

Kerrie and Kimmy were both involved with the Cheer and Dance Program while attending UNR. After graduation, Kimmy returned to the University to become Head Coach of the cheerleading program. Kerrie spent some time after college working for a floral business. Now and then she privately creates designs for weddings and parties, but she really enjoys her full-time job at Name Droppers. She liked Mia's shop so much, it seemed only logical they should work together.

Mia's most memorable event concerning her shop was in 2002, when she asked Kerrie to be her manager. Kerrie has a flair for design. Her intuition for knowing what new items will be the next big seller is a tremendous asset. Mia and Kerrie try to go to wholesale buyers' markets together several times a year.

Mia was thrilled in April of 2000 to have Pam, Kimmy and Kerrie join Andy at her bedside at St. Mary's Hospital for the birth of their son, Jack. A few years later, Kimmy gave birth to Mia's darling twin nieces, Addison and Kenedi. Another baby girl, named Whitney, followed in the fall of 2005. With three small inquisitive children to run after, Kimmy still finds time to stop by the store and keep Mia up-to-date on family events.

The sisters' kinship is ingrained in their beings; there is no other way to explain it. Their sisterhood has worked out better than Mia ever expected, and she feels completely at ease with them. Perhaps it has something to do with being the youngest in the Brophy family, versus having more confidence as the oldest sister in the Anastassatos family. Whatever the reason, Mia is grateful to have such wonderful, spirited sisters, and knows it is a great tribute to Pam and Angelo for raising such terrific daughters.

Emmy, Gilly, and Jack were thrilled to participate in their Aunt Kerrie's elegant wedding to Jesse Hon on New Year's Eve, 2008.

During the last several years, Mia's "what-ifs" have finally been put to rest. She knew Kimmy and Kerrie didn't have to like her or even want to meet her. Do they argue and disagree now and then? Of course, but that's what makes it real. "I just love saying 'my sisters,' over and over. My real blood sisters," Mia says to anyone who will listen.

Pam and Angelo call Mia "daughter." It feels right. As with her newfound sisters, Mia knows it was a real possibility they could have rejected her. She meant every word she wrote in her letter to Pam and Angelo, and they have taken Mia at her word. Mia feels she started off by turning Pam's life upside-down when Pam was pregnant, and then she came around and upset her life for a second time. Catholic guilt, but guilt nonetheless—it affects Mia and is a fine thread that runs through her personality.

Deep in her heart, Mia always had a longing for a huge family. She couldn't explain it, let alone discuss it with anyone. But she just knew that somewhere, she had biological aunts, uncles, and cousins. Her newfound aunts are Sophia, Maria, and Alex. The uncles are Spiros, Jerry, Dennis, and George. Mia yearned to meet them and dreamed of the times when they could have family reunions and get together to celebrate marriages, births, and anniversaries. Never in her wildest thoughts did she imagine they would almost all live in the same community and that she would be embraced as part of their family.

Getting On With Her Life

THE ONE PERSON WHO benefits from this book is Mia. Sharing her account of the adoption has been therapeutic for her, to say the least. It has, in fact, filled the void she had in her life. I spent many an afternoon and evening listening to her recall the unique events leading up to her discovery. Mia told me she opened a box, not Pandora's Box, but a beautiful gift box, like one you would find in her store. She will never regret it. The box contained many mixed emotions that she needed to release, along with many happy, unexpected surprises.

Emmy is now a high school teenager, Gilly is getting ready for middle school, and Jack is enjoying his elementary school classes. All three are remarkable students and look forward to classroom challenges as well as opportunities to learn new sports.

The girls were wonderful and approached the whole discovery with the enthusiasm and honesty only children can bestow. Their natural curiosity was illuminating to watch and their acceptance of a new and greatly enlarged family seemed only natural to them. Jack was born into the completed family and never knew anything different.

Remarkable family stories of people and events are now a part of Mia's newly discovered history and future. The people she met along the way who shared their insights have all enriched her life, from the social worker at the adoption agency, to recently found relatives, to past friends of her adoptive mom and dad.

D'Arcy frequently reminds Mia of all the crazy antics they shared as brother and sister; memories of floating down the narrow irrigation canal behind their Circle Drive home on rafts they made, and the wonderful summer vacations at their family's enclave off, of Vancouver Island in Canada.

D'Arcy has succeeded in establishing his own notoriety within the local medical community as an orthopedic assistant surgeon. He and Mia get together as often as their schedules allow. Emmy, Gilly, and Jack adore their Uncle D'Arcy. "Our parents and Ga would have been so proud of him," Mia says.

Mia told me her mom and dad had complex views on rearing their children, but without them, she wouldn't be the person she is today. They taught her right from wrong, indulged her, coached her on good manners, provided her with a Christian upbringing, and loved her deeply. At times she misses the formality of her early home life. As a sign of the times growing up in the 1960s and 1970s, the family ate in the dining room every night while listening to classical music, and shared stories of the day's events with the frequent guests invited to join them for dinner. Mia attributes her fondness for dinner parties and enter-taining to her mom and Grandma Ga. She realizes that her social skills and also her tendency toward privacy were ingrained into her being by her adoptive parents. They are why she is here and is the resilient person she is today.

The Quinn side of Mia's family offered guidance and support, while encouraging Mia to keep her sense of humor and not take herself too seriously. David, her father-in-law, spoke with a level-headed knowledge and balance that Mia drew upon time and again. Being a former banker and a stockbroker has given him a unique awareness and understanding of people.

At first, Mia kept her idea of finding her parents to herself, but because the events culminated quickly, she turned to close friends and family for moral support and suggestions on how to proceed. We talked on several occasions about how best to approach these newly found relatives, in consideration of their privacy. Full of excitement, Mia was determined to reach a mutually beneficial conclusion.

Andy was by Mia's side at each turn of events. He warned her to tread lightly, and celebrated with her at the eventual discovery. Andy has found her journey unbelievable and is proud of Mia for sticking with her dream.

Just after her discovery, friends Kelli Newman, Mary Ellen Arrascada, Ardis Parmer, and Tammy Ernst helped Mia through some rough spots. They were a sounding board she depended on to give her objective answers as circumstances unfolded around her.

Mia loves reading and enjoys spending a few stolen moments in her favorite local bookstore whenever she can. "Mia, you really need to write a book and share your story with others," people would tell her. The idea took a few years to gel, but Mia realized how helpful and encouraging it might be for people in her same situation.

Mia's older sister Patricia was instrumental in creating this book. She was able to remember Mia's mom and dad in the years before Mia became a part of the Brophy family. Mia and I bombarded Patricia with all sorts of questions. She took the project to heart, as we knew she would, and shared her many thoughts. She spoke of the adoptions of Linda, D'Arcy and Mia as non-issues, the outlook the entire Brophy family had shared during Mia's childhood. Patricia, a former nun, lives in Reno with her husband, Richard Eisenberg, and their son John. Mia's sister Linda has three children and lives in the Midwest. Mia and Linda have never spoken of their adoptions. Sue has gone her separate way, and Mia has not heard from her in years.

Back Row: Andy & Mia Quinn, Kerrie, Kimmy & Mark
Welker
Middle: Gilly Quinn, Angelo, Pam, Emmy Quinn
Front: Addison Welker, Jack Quinn, Kenedi Welker

The Best Is Yet To Come

Soon after Mia's story started to circulate about town, friends as well as complete strangers confided in her that they were also adopted and looking for their birth parents. Some questioned Mia about the steps she took to find her birth parents and asked for her advice. She realizes, without a doubt, how exceedingly fortunate she was in her pursuit. The pieces of the puzzle literally fell into her lap.

Even today, the issue of adoption can be explosive. Mia knows of individuals, right here in Reno, who have taken the proper legal steps by going through the courts, attorneys, and adoption agencies, only to be turned away, unable to get any help. Sadly, records and files are often closed. Mia feels that if adopted children are raised in a home where they are treated as equals, with love and respect, that will be a glowing beacon guiding them in their quest to find their own birth history. Some adopted people will feel an inexplicable urge to reach out to birth parents, while others will be content with the status quo.

Moral issues were challenged when Mia chose to enter, unannounced, into her birth parents' lives. Volumes have been written on this subject by learned psychologists, sociologists, and medical doctors. The limited information available to adopted people seems to exclude them from their own pasts, telling them to "please be understanding," protecting the biological couple and adoptive parents first and foremost. In some ways they seem to be told, "You should just be glad you were adopted and placed in a home instead of an orphanage. Now stop complaining and get on with your life." Mia acknowledges this harsh point of view, but agrees it fails to help the deep emotions of the adoptee, and basically reaches no conclusions.

In the era in which Mia was raised, the subject of adoption was never discussed. Perhaps that is still true today, to some degree. Children like Mia have grown up feeling they are part of a big secret. As an adopted child, you might be convinced you're breaking a rule by thinking about those "other people," those phantoms from your past. But you're really not.

Some might view Mia's decision as selfish—but what about her "right to know"? None of the circumstances leading up to her birth and adoption were her idea. What's more, she had no hidden agenda in searching for her birth parents, except to uncover the truth and discover her medical history for the benefit of her children. Her experience turned out to be more than she ever expected, and she hopes others have a successful outcome, should they decide to do their own investigation.

Mia has no regrets, and realizes she was very fortunate. It was God's plan. Mia truly believes this. The events that unfolded around her seemed to be spiritually guided. She now knows the truth of her adoption. She has a peace within and a sense of accomplishment. Mia took the necessary steps and found out her missing history. Her life can now move forward in a positive way, with no more secrets from her past. Mia is very thankful to everyone involved in the successful outcome. The hidden puzzle pieces have been found, and the adoption quandary she struggled with for so long is now at peace.

The Second Beginning...

Acknowledgements

MANY INDIVIDUALS HAVE BEEN helpful in developing this book. Friends who were gracious and volunteered to read my first draft are retired *Los Angeles Times* journalist Earl Gustkey, screenwriter Pam Dulgar, White House advisor to President Ronald Reagan, Ty Cobb and his wife Suellen, Janice and Hal Plummer and Merle and Phil Rose.

To George Vicari, who started me off with a cup of coffee, encouragement, and several books at Barnes and Noble to help keep me on track, thank you. Mike Sion, your notes were a big help. I express my appreciation to published writer and long time friend, Karl Breckenridge who gave me an insight into the world of publishing.

A special debt of gratitude to Patty Caffereta and Kim Henrick, published writers and members of the

Unnamed Writers Group of Northern Nevada for their critiques and constructive criticism.

Two enjoyable interviews with Patricia Brophy Eisenberg and John D'Arcy Brophy helped me understand Mia's early years with the Brophy family.

I spent several delightful afternoons with Spiros Anastassatos and his sisters Maria Anastassatos Aramini and Sophia Anastassatos Diotallezi, as they shared fascinating tales of their family history in Greece.

Thank you to Kimmy and Kerrie, for being the best sisters Mia could wish for.

I appreciate so much the generosity of Pam and Angelo, who shared their private memories, without which this story couldn't have been told.

I am grateful for the continued support and encouragement of my husband Dave and our daughter Kathy, throughout the several years it has taken me to write this book.

To copy editors Chris Wanzer, for helping with my first draft, and Linda Jay Geldens, who saw me through to the final page, I am indebted. Both women were there for me when I needed it most, with kindness, keen insights, and endurance.

Mia responded with a loving and generous heart to my never ending questions. Thank you, so much for sharing these tender memories and delightful stories.

Photo Credits

COVER PHOTO OF MIA Quinn courtesy of CLEVER Magazine and Photographer Linda Reeve of Reno, Nevada.

Vaughn Hartung at Hartung & Dickman in Sparks, Nevada for the back cover photo of Sharon Quinn and for making digital magic with the collection of old family photos.

Chris Armitage wedding photo of Angelo and Pam Anastassatos, Reno, Nevada

Bret Hofman wedding photo of Mia and Andy Quinn, Reno, Nevada

Portraiture of Gilly, Jack and Emmy Quinn by Precious Treasures, Kristen Echeverria-La Bella, Reno, Nevada

About The Author

SHARON LYMAN QUINN GREW up in Newport Beach, California and studied business at the University of Nevada, Reno. Developing an interest in writing at an early age Sharon had her own weekly newspaper column in the Newport Harbor News-Press and was assistant editor of her college yearbook.

A lifelong community volunteer, Sharon has served on the Truckee Meadows Community College Foundation Board of Nevada, Reno Philharmonic Board, co-developed the Reno, Nevada, Ronald McDonald House and is active in the arts. Married to Dave Quinn, her college sweetheart, Sharon has two children and five grandchildren.

Besides taking time out from her 30 years as a Realtor to write about her daughter in law, Mia, in Second Beginning, Sharon enjoys travel, art museums, gardening, and watching old movies. She is currently working on an historic novel set near Boston in 1675.

Printed in the United States
123580LV00001B/142-378/P